COACHING YOUTH NETBALL

An Essential Guide for Coaches, Parents and Teachers

Anita Navin

THE CROWOOD PRESS

First published in 2016 by
The Crowood Press Ltd
Ramsbury, Marlborough
Wiltshire SN8 2HR

www.crowood.com

British Library Cataloguing-in-Publication Data
A catalogue record for this book is available from the British Library.

ISBN 978 1 78500 116 1

Dedication
This book is dedicated to all those club volunteers who work tirelessly to
promote the game of netball at youth level.

Acknowledgements
The editor, authors and publishers would like to thank Laura Woodrow, a
photography student at the University of Gloucestershire, for her willingness
and support in kindly providing photographs for this publication. Thanks go to
Hucclecote Netball Club players and coaches for allowing the photographer to
attend the junior club session. In addition the editor is grateful for the supply of
photographs for both chapters and cover from the appointed England Netball
photographer, David Kitchin (www.takethatfoto.co.uk).

Typeset by Jean Cussons Typesetting, Diss, Norfolk
Printed and bound in India by Replika Pres Pvt Ltd

CONTENTS

CONTRIBUTOR PROFILES

Dr Anita Navin (editor)

Anita is currently the Head of School for Sport and Exercise at the University of Gloucestershire. Anita was a teacher of Physical Education and was successful in the development of netball for the U18 age groups as part of her role in secondary education. Coaching teams at national finals and promoting netball for fitness and a healthy lifestyle remained priorities throughout her career in schools. Anita has been involved with England Netball for over twenty-five years as an athlete, coach, coach developer, talent scout and a lead consultant for the development of both education and coach mentoring programmes. In 2011 Anita was awarded the UK Coach Educator of the Year and has continued to support the development of coaching at all levels. Anita was a high performance coach for England Netball, working closely with age group and senior athletes on a weekly basis at the home training centres. Internationally Anita has taken on a lead coaching role with Netball Northern Ireland. In addition she has held an Assistant Coach position and Director of Netball role with the Team Northumbria Franchise in the England Netball Super League. Anita is a highly experienced coach and coach educator and her involvement in the strategic development of sport and sports coaching contributed to her appointment onto the following:

- UK Sport World Class Coaching Steering Group

- The International Netball Federation's Coaching Advisory Group
- Sports Coach UK Coaching Standards Group.

Anita continued her support of netball in the performance context following her selection to a commentary role with the Sky Sports channel in 2006 and is still actively involved as a pundit and commentator for the programme. Anita has been part of the commentary team for all of the England International Test matches, and was appointed by the host broadcaster to commentate at the Commonwealth Games in Glasgow in 2014 and the Netball World Cup in Australia in 2015. Anita has supported the development of netball in Africa and devised a Level 1 qualification programme for coaches on behalf of the INF (International Netball Federation). In addition Anita completed her Professional Doctorate, which investigated the characteristics of expertise in coaches within netball. With The Crowood Press, Anita has published a range of texts on netball and sports coaching.

Nicky Fuller

Nicky Fuller is a coaching consultant, working with a range of national governing bodies and their coaches. She supports in the development of qualification programmes (UKCC Levels 1–4) and on-going professional development workshops. She works with individual coaches from netball, equestrian disciplines and golf to develop their professional expertise. Her formal association with England Netball started when she was selected to represent the country in junior age group squads. Over the years she has become a coach, umpire, development officer and administrator within England Netball. Her coaching has taken her to work with the national side of Dominica in the Caribbean and across the UK. Most recently her interest has been in coaching junior netballers at Club and County Academy. She jointly founded her current junior netball club in Shropshire, which has been developing over the past twelve years with squads from U11 to U19. She is passionate about using netball as a tool to develop the personal skills of girls and young women.

Alison Croad

Alison is currently a Senior Lecturer in Sports Coaching at the University of Gloucestershire, where she is also Head of Netball. Alison's main research interests include innovative approaches to coaching and the impact of coach development on coaching practice. Her latest study investigated the implementation of game-based coaching pedagogy in elite performance sport, exploring the process of elite coaching and the development of player autonomy. Alongside her academic role, Alison is a keen sports person: having previously competed internationally in athletics, she now plays netball and has coached within a range of different sporting environments. These include primary and secondary schools and the County Netball Academy. Through her previous employment Alison worked as a community sports coach and then as a coaching manager with the local county sports partnership. Alison has also contributed to the International Netball Federation's net-

ball development programme by supporting an event in Ethiopia. Alison delivered a range of sessions to teachers of Physical Education where a game-based pedagogy was adopted.

Jose Castro

Jose is a Lecturer in Sports Coaching at the University of Gloucestershire, and his teaching commitments are focused on sports coaching and research methods. His main research interests relate to coach and player learning, through the application of pedagogical approaches within the coaching setting. In fact, Jose's doctoral study investigates coach and athlete learning in team sports, using a game-based approach which encourages coaches and players to critically reflect on the game's tactical constraints, promoting decision-making and, consequently, performance. Alongside his academic role, Jose is also an experienced international volleyball coach and was recently awarded 'Coach of the Year' by the South West Volleyball Association and 'Performance Development Coach of Year 2014' by the England Volleyball Association. Additionally, Jose is a Sports Coach UK qualified Tutor, and Volleyball England Tutor.

Maggie Jackson

Maggie Jackson is a former Physical Education teacher and is currently working both in education and in coaching. Maggie, a former international netball player, is involved in the England Netball High Performance Programme as a National Selector and a mentor for potential Level 3 and High Performance Coaches. She was the Head Coach for Hertfordshire Mavericks for six years, where they successfully reached the final each year and won the

Netball Super League Competition on two occasions. With Maggie as the Interim Head Coach at the 2010 Commonwealth Games and Assistant Coach in the 2006 Commonwealth Games and the 2011 World Cup, the England squads achieved third place in all competitions. Maggie is an accredited tutor with England Netball and regularly delivers workshops and UKCC courses. She was awarded an MBE in 2012 for Services to Netball.

Denise Egan

Denise is a consultant in Sports Coaching and is actively engaged in promoting expertise in netball coaching through a range of programmes. Denise was previously an Assistant Headteacher in a secondary school and has supported the development of trainee and newly-qualified teachers of Physical Education. Denise is a successful World Championships and Commonwealth Games coach for England Netball and was one of the first coaches to run a high performance netball programme for the North of England. She is also renowned for putting forward successful teams in National Schools Netball competitions and her notable achievements include eight players from the school gaining a place in the England Netball squads. Currently, Denise is also an active coach educator for England Netball as part of their UK Coaching Certification programme.

Gary Burgess

Gary Burgess is one of the world's leading netball officials, umpiring the 2010 and 2014 Commonwealth Games Gold Medal matches and the 2011 and 2015 Netball World Cup Finals. Domestically he has umpired the last eight Netball Super League Finals. A leader in umpire education, Gary writes regularly for the publication *Netball* and has worked extensively throughout the British Isles and Europe as an advisor to National Umpiring Associations. Away from Netball Gary is currently an Assistant Principal at a large comprehensive school in Norfolk.

Jane Lomax

Jane is currently a Senior Lecturer at the University of Chichester, training sports coaches, Physical Education teachers and adventure educators. She is a BASES accredited sports science support worker in psychology with over twenty years' experience working with performers and coaches from a range of sports, including five seasons with England Netball squads. Jane's coaching experience within netball includes English and British universities, National Talent League teams, as well as working with younger players at school, club and county level. Jane is a tutor, assessor, internal verifier and mentor for England Netball's coach education programme and currently sits on the High Performance and Coaching Advisory Groups. Jane also has experience in coaching other sports including skiing; teaching within the secondary sector; management training within the corporate world and has spent many years tutoring for Sports Coach UK.

Penny Rumbold

Dr Penny Rumbold is a Lecturer in Sport and Exercise Nutrition in the Department of Sport and Exercise Sciences at Northumbria University. Her teaching interests lie primarily in the nutritional and physiological aspects of sport, exercise and health, and also paediatric exercise physiology. Through her PhD work Penny focused on energy and appetite regulation in young athletes involved in netball. Penny competed in netball and her passion for the sport meant she supported coaching in her community-based club in Tyne and Wear.

Abbe Brady

Abbe is based at the University of Gloucestershire, where she is presently the Course Leader for the MSc Sports Coaching and the Professional Doctorate in Sport and Exercise. Alongside her academic role Abbe is a BASES accredited Sport Scientist and an HCPC registered Sport and Exercise Psychologist, through which she supports coaches and athletes to develop and flourish in the pursuit of their respective goals. Over the last twenty years Abbe has worked in the design and delivery of coach and mentor education for sports coach UK and national governing bodies in sport and more recently her work has extended to business settings. Abbe's research interests in coaching include: practices associated with athlete and coach well-being; examining coach resilience, and how coaches support the development of strengths, resilience and positive psychological capital in athletes; exploring humanization and holistic practice within coaching and

leadership; developing cultures that promote growth mind-set, and the efficacy of reflective practice and mentoring in coach development.

Barbara Daniels

Barbara is an independent coach education consultant who has worked in sports such as cricket and netball in developing their UKCC qualifications and in training coaches and coach developers. She played cricket for England from 1993 to 2000 and was Executive Director of the Women's Cricket Association and, subsequently, the National Manager for women's cricket for the England and Wales Cricket Board (ECB). She is currently working with the PGA on developing and delivering their Level 3 coach education programme and is studying for an MPhil at the University of Gloucestershire. In recent years she has been mentoring coaches through their Level 3 and 4 qualifications and has become an international mentor for coaches in Olympic and Paralympic sports from smaller Olympic nations. She is also involved in the delivery of the Women in Sports Leadership programme run through the Anita White Foundation and the University of Chichester. Barbara's research interests are in coach learning and reflective practice.

CHAPTER 1

INTRODUCTION TO COACHING YOUTH PARTICIPANTS

Anita Navin

Successful coaching of children is associated with positive participant outcomes such as enjoyment, the promotion of intrinsic motivation and self-esteem. Effective coaches know all the techniques and tactics within the game of netball and will be able to demonstrate the ability to individualize communication and activities based on the needs of the participant. Effective coaching is not only related to the development of netball or game-specific outcomes, but is connected to the all-round holistic development of the

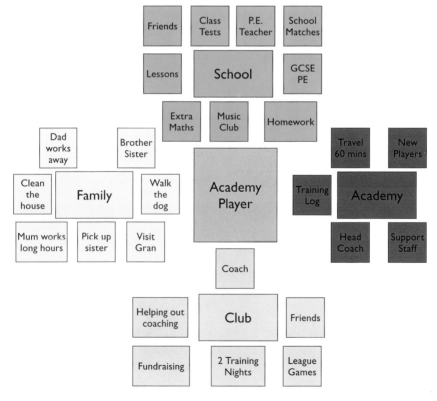

Fig. 1.1 The potential pressures and demands placed on a young participant.

individual. Successful coaching in the youth context should not be driven by winning but should prioritize the holistic development of the young person.

There can be many influential factors underpinning a young person's behaviour, motives and individual needs when they enter into a coaching session and it is therefore important to build a relationship with the individual. Fig. 1.1 offers an example of a young person's commitments both within and outside netball. The coach should develop an understanding of any family or education demands that can impact upon the individual in a coaching context. In addition, if a participant is a member of a performance development pathway there will be added netball demands from another context.

A participant-centred and holistic coach will develop trusting working relationships with each individual and most of all will have an insight into the lifestyle demands of each person. Acknowledging an individual's potential is vital, and ensuring the needs of the person are known and met is critical to success in the coaching role.

A humanistic approach in coaching is essential, where the total development of the participant is a priority. A coach will focus on enhancing self-awareness, growth and development of the participant, ensuring each individual is engaged in decision-making within a session. To facilitate the attainment of such humanistic outcomes, the coach will empower participants by asking a range of open questions to engage and prompt ownership of the learning process. In addition, participants will be encouraged to work collaboratively and foster a team climate for learning. The coach must provide a safe and supportive environment for learning, enabling the young person to make personal choices. Supporting a participant's ideas and self-expression are important factors for the humanistic-

Understanding individual needs within the group is critical in coaching.

focused coach. There are several assumptions connected to the humanistic approach and coaches are encouraged to model each and every one in their coaching practice.

It is therefore not just about the development of sport-specific outcomes; the coach should promote the development of the young participant as an authentic and valued individual. When coaching young novice participants there will be greater coach control and coach dependency. As the individual develops competence and confidence there should be opportunities provided for self-management, self-determination and shared decision-making. A primary aim of any coach is to ensure there is a shift in coach dependency as an individual develops, in order to ultimately promote per-

Individuals should be encouraged to work collaboratively within a session.

sonal autonomy and participant independence.

Coaching effectiveness has also been defined by the participant outcomes a coach should strive for when supporting the development of the young participant. Known as the '4Cs' – competence, confidence, connection and character (Côté and Gilbert, 2009) – the outcomes should be a reference for all coaches in the youth context. (Sports

ASSUMPTIONS OF A HUMANISTIC APPROACH

- Competition goals should not take priority over personalized goals and the needs of the individual.
- A coach should promote an individual's development through empowerment, engagement and self-determination.
- Netball will be only a part of an individual's life, so a coach should consider this in relation to other human experiences such as family, career, education and health.
- Coaching should focus not only on the technical and tactical aspects of the sport but on emotional, social and psychological performance.
- Coaching should be built around successful interpersonal and professional relationships between the coach and participant.

The four Cs – representing the outcomes of effective coaching in netball:

Competence   Technical and tactical skills of the game, improved health and fitness and healthy training habits.

Confidence   Overall positive self-worth.

Connection   Positive bonds and social relationships with people inside and outside netball.

Character   Respect for the sport and others (morality), integrity, empathy and responsibility.

Coach UK offer '5Cs', developed from the work of Jean Côté, which includes Creativity, and the five Cs are referred to later in the text.)

Coaches should always ensure they have a clear philosophy representing a set of values to underpin their coaching behaviour and practice. Successful coaches will be self-aware and will 'know themselves' through the ability to self-reflect on their coaching. This self-reflection should closely connect with your own philosophy, remaining as a guide for coaching practice and making sure you as the coach remain true to yourself. A coaching philosophy is often a statement of the beliefs and values that coaches will model their coaching practice upon. When difficult decisions have to be made in the coaching role, it is the philosophy that should be used to underpin the outcome.

Developing Your Coaching Philosophy

All coaches will possess values they believe explain their actions in both life and coaching. For example, if a coach values hard work and effort in a session, rewards will be based on this commitment and maximum effort. Other values may include respect, health, honesty, self-responsibility, trust, friendships and enjoyment. Coaches should uphold their values and model them in everyday life to ensure they impact positively on all individuals they come into contact with. Having a positive influence physically, psychologically and socially are important considerations for the youth coach. An example of a coaching philosophy for a coach in netball is outlined below:

AN EXAMPLE OF A COACH PHILOSOPHY

As a coach I will create an environment where there is mutual respect between the coach and participants. I will promote openness, honesty and equity at all times and I will be accountable for all that I do. I will educate participants to become independent and strive to ensure everyone reaches his or her true potential. I will remain committed to ongoing learning and development to maintain currency in the coaching role.

As a result of additional experiences in the coaching role your beliefs may change, so it is important to modify your philosophy. Reflect upon your coaching practice to ensure that there is a match with your philosophy. A philosophy should influence coaching practice and an individual's coach development pathway.

Coaching Process Skills

The coaching process or craft-based skills provide a set of guiding principles for the delivery of an effective coaching session. A coach must have knowledge of technical and tactical components impacting upon performance, along with the necessary communication and interpersonal skills, to be successful. A coach who is a technical expert or most conscientious and effective in the planning phase will only succeed if the craft-based skills are applied in the delivery of the coaching session. Effective organization of the working environment and good communication skills contribute to individual satisfaction and performance improvement within the sports setting.

It is the 'how to' coach skills which provide strategies and which are an essential 'tool kit' for the coach. The 'how to coach' skills reviewed in this chapter provide guidance on creating a positive climate, the organization of resources, presentation of information and coach relationships/interventions with the participants.

THE 'HOW TO COACH' SKILLS

- Safety
- Building rapport
- Fun
- Organization
- Explanation
- Demonstration
- Observation
- Analysis
- Feedback

Creating a Positive Environment

Safety

Initially the coach must ensure that the working environment is free from hazards and risks. In addition the coach should assess the risks within the coaching environment by considering the participants, the intended activity, the equipment, coaching methods and the working environment. An evaluation and overall assessment of the risks should take place and often a Risk Assessment proforma utilized by the coach would identify the impact of the risk in terms of a rating of low, medium to high. The rating relates to the likelihood of the risk leading to an injury and the frequency at which the coach believes this could occur. The coach is required to make a decision in relation to the intended action and most often the coach will eliminate the risk from the coaching environment. If the risk cannot be eliminated, the coach must accept the risk and implement an approach to safeguard all participants. A coach will decide to either avoid the activity due to the high risk factor with a particular group and associated environment or accept the risk and work to the safe practice principles outlined in this chapter. Reinforcing the safety issues with participants and conveying the code of behaviour for them to work to will support the coach in ensuring safe and effective practice.

Environment

The coach should perform a check of the

Step 1: Identify the risks
Step 2: Evaluate the risks
Step 3: Select an approach to manage the risk
Step 4: Implement the approach

Promoting a safe environment for player development is essential.

working space. The following guidelines identify the specific aspects a coach should consider prior to, during and after the coaching session:

- Check for any debris on or around the working area.
- Ensure there is access to a telephone in case of emergency.
- Know the first aid procedure at the venue.
- If outdoors, monitor the temperature.
- The weather can affect the outdoor working area; check the surface, particularly if there has been rain, frost or falling leaves.
- Secure all fixed equipment and store equipment not in use.
- Ensure lighting is adequate.
- Check emergency exits are not obstructed and fire procedures are known.
- Ensure participants know how to carry the piece of equipment safely.

- The coach should always check any equipment that has been assembled by others prior to using it.
- Always communicate the working area and boundaries to the participants within the session.
- Ensure equipment is appropriate to the age and ability level of the group.
- Store equipment intended for use in a safe place during the session.
- Distribute equipment in a safe and systematic form, making sure large numbers do not all descend on an equipment store or one location to collect equipment at any one time.
- Ensure equipment is put away safely at the end of the session and participants follow the routines communicated by the coach.

Participants
A coach should carry out a check with all individuals in terms of their readiness to partici-

pate. It is essential that the coach is briefed and informed of any injuries or illness a participant may have sustained and that asthmatic participants have their inhalers with them at all times. The participants should remove all jewellery, tie long hair back away from the face and should be wearing appropriate clothing and footwear for the session. Participants must not be allowed to chew gum during the session, but all should be encouraged to have water bottles with them for rehydrating. During the session a coach must ensure that no young person leaves the session and is unsupervised.

All planned activities and progressions should be appropriate to the individuals in a session, and to promote a safe and productive working environment the coach should establish and reinforce rules and safe practice routines with the participants.

Building Rapport

Interpersonal skills are of paramount importance, given the complexities of human interaction that feature within the coaching environment. A coach should get to know the participants, appreciate their needs and individual differences, acknowledge their efforts and be an active listener. Active listening enhances communication and the coach should pay full attention to the speaker, make eye contact with the participants and use a nodding gesture to demonstrate understanding. A coach who actively listens may summarize what has been said with lead-in questions to the speaker, for example, 'What you are telling me is…'

A coach should make every effort to speak with all participants in a session and show respect to everyone irrespective of their ability level. The power of non-verbal communication, e.g. a smile, must not be underestimated; a coach who smiles and engages with participants is more likely to create

SAFETY

- Assess risks associated with the participants, environment and equipment.
- A coach should perform the same checks throughout a session.
- Ensure participants remain 'on task' and in the correct area.
- Ensure the learning activities and progressions are appropriate.

a supportive climate for learning. A coach should also bear in mind that up to 70 per cent of communication is often defined as non-verbal.

Fun

The 'fun factor' must not be underestimated within a coaching session. While a productive and safe environment must be maintained, fun practices and activities will motivate and engage participants. To make a session fun the coach should apply the good practice principles outlined below:

Ensure participants are active quickly
- Know your session plan.
- Equipment is organized and easily accessed.
- Plan explanations and use cue words to reduce talk time.
- Participants should have all they need for the session (kit, drinks bottle and personal equipment required).

Learning activities should be varied and challenging for all
- Differentiate your planning for all performance levels.
- Avoid repetition of the same warm-up, practice and groupings.

Engaging and developing rapport with a young group will promote a positive environment.

- Make a conscious effort to offer a novel idea or different task in each session planned.

Promote activities for all participants to be actively involved
- Keep group sizes small to reduce any waiting time in long queues.
- Plan for odd numbers in the practices.
- Equipment should be organized for the numbers in the session.
- Make adaptations if an individual is repeatedly over- or under-challenged on a task.

Feedback should be positive and reward effort along with performance outcomes
- Praise individuals who commit fully to the task and always give of their best in a session.
- If there is an error in terms of performance, offer corrective feedback or open questions to tease out what the individual should do.

Organization

A coach must be an effective organizer of all resources, and this is a vital consideration within the planning phase. Coaches must plan how they will manage the participants, support coaches, the working area and equipment. An effective coach will also have a contingency or back-up plan should there be fewer or more participants, a reduced working area or indeed problems with equipment. When organizing individuals into groups and allocating working areas, the coach should strive for smooth transitions between practices and re-groupings. Effective organization will address the following issues:

Planning
- Know the number of participants and note how you will run a practice with more or fewer participants.
- Clearly note how the working area will be sectioned and try to maintain similar set-

ups, therefore maximizing the time spent in a learning activity.
- Plan the process for allocating or collecting equipment in a session.
- Complete any organizational steps prior to a group arriving for the session if possible.

Safety considerations
- Complete a risk assessment for a coaching venue.
- Check the working area before commencing delivery of a session.
- Do not use any faulty equipment.
- Reduce the area of work if there are hazards close by.

A coach must be an effective organizer of resources in a session.

Grouping participants
- Organize groups randomly or by ability.
- Be sensitive when grouping by ability and set realistic challenges for each group accordingly.
- Plan groups in advance and progress logically (e.g. 2s to 4s, 3s to 6s).

Group size
- Consider the intensity and involvement of all participants.
- Smaller groups maximize involvement.
- If the activity is intensive a larger group offers more recovery/rest time, thus encouraging high quality practice.
- Smaller groups contain fewer communication channels between participants, therefore any discussion is easier.

Explanation

Success as a coach manifests itself in the art of communication and a coach must understand how to send an effective message to participants. A breakdown in communication is often the result of the content (too much/too little) of the information being communicated, misinterpretation, or as a result of the coach not communicating sufficient information. The content of the message should be appropriate to the age level of the participants and user-friendly language should be used. A coach should plan what is to be communicated and ensure all participants are attentive and free from distraction. Explanations should be simple, brief and direct and a coach should use appropriate questioning to check for understanding at the end of an explanation. Exemplar questions to check for understanding at the end of an explanation are noted below:

- What will you now focus upon in the practice?
- How many in each group?

- Where will players stand to start the practice?

A coach should avoid asking the question 'Do you understand?' as this will often prompt individuals to respond with a 'yes' even though they require more information. Participants often feel reluctant to expose their lack of understanding in a whole group context and a coach should avoid such exposure by asking appropriately worded questions.

Demonstration

Demonstrations present a visual picture of the task organization/practice context and the technical/tactical information to be learned. A demonstration along with a concise explanation will often be connected together and can be used before participants practise a skill, intermittently throughout the skill development phase or as a conclusion to a particular practice or phase in the session.

The explanation when combined with a demonstration should be concise and incorporate learning cues, often referred to as a key word or phrase that summarizes and identifies the main features of a skill or task. The learning cues presented must be appropriate to age and experience, and be concise and accurate in order to assist the individual in the learning process. A coach may decide to breakdown a skill into the three phases of preparation, execution and recovery in order to identify the key learning cues. Using action words or verbal labels can assist participants and support retention of key information.

The demonstration is deemed to be one of the most important sources of self-efficacy information for a novice or intermediate performer. Observing a fellow participant complete a demonstration of a difficult task can reduce anxiety for others. In order to fully understand the importance of demonstra-

Success in coaching is dependent upon the ability to communicate with participants.

tion, a four-stage process has been outlined below:

Attention
- Ensure all participants can see, hear and are free from distraction (e.g. not facing the sun, other activities, etc.).
- Introduce the skill to focus the participants and gain interest.
- As the coach, direct attention to the key elements of the skill.
- Focus upon one or two key points or cues.

Retention
- The demonstration should be observed more than once and from different angles if required.

- Question participants on the key points/ cues given to check for understanding.
- A coach should repeat the same cues with each demonstration to improve retention.

Reproduction
- A coach must plan appropriate progressions following a demonstration to support the performer.
- Individuals may not be able to perform the skill being demonstrated due to not having developed the pre-requisite skills.
- A coach must continue to reinforce the key points and allocate ample time to practise the skill immediately after the demonstration.
- Slow-motion demonstrations may be useful in the early stages of learning.
- Observing a demonstration of someone not performing as an expert may prompt observational learning and allow the observer to engage in the problem-solving processes the performer would be experiencing.

Motivation
- Individuals may lack the motivation to learn a new skill, but if the demonstrator has a high level of skill, social status and competence the participant is likely to be attentive.
- A coach should praise participants and communicate the importance and relevance of the skill being demonstrated.
- The demonstration should be timed to prevent too much standing around.

When planning a demonstration the coach must carefully consider how the participants will be organized. Often a coach will ensure all equipment and the working areas for each group have been set up before the demonstration. A coach may elect to use one of the following arrangements to deliver a demonstration, ensuring all participants can see from the same angle:

- semi-circle formation
- group standing at the side line of the court area
- group positioned around a key area of the court, e.g. shooting circle

Consideration must be given to the viewpoint of the participants; the positioning of the coach in relation to the group can impact upon the clarity of the demonstration. A coach who stands in close proximity to a group may reduce the visibility of the demonstration for some participants. When arranged in a semi-circle formation, the coach who stands too close will be viewed from the side by the individuals standing at the end of the semi-circle but from the front by those standing in the middle.

When evaluating the success of a demonstration the coach should utilize the following review questions to prompt accurate self-reflection.

- Were the organizational issues related to equipment, participant groupings and the working areas covered prior to the demonstration?
- Was the purpose of the demonstration communicated clearly?
- What were the coaching points communicated in the demonstration?
- Was the organization also communicated in the demonstration?
- Was the demonstration a good model of the movement? Why?
- How was the group arranged to view the demonstration?
- How did the coach conclude the demonstration?

- Was the transition time between demonstration and practice time minimal? Why?

Observation

Following a demonstration a coach must facilitate the learning process; this is an essential skill that is necessary for giving quality feedback. Effective observation relates closely to movement analysis and a coach should do the following: plan how to observe (from different angles, see the action more than once); make a decision on what to observe and identify the critical features; and understand the factors that impact upon one's ability to observe e.g. skill level, number of participants, size of the working area, fear and personal knowledge).

Observing performance with a large number of participants can prove challenging, and coaches are encouraged to focus on one coaching point or learning cue as they move around the group. The learning cue or coaching point selected should be one that was covered in the demonstration and explanation of the skill. The coach must have a mental picture of the perfect model of the skill or task and use this to form the basis of any observations. The coach will be non-judgemental at this stage and will build up an overview of what is being observed. Once this information has been obtained the coach is able to diagnose the performance.

Analysis

Following the observation stage, a coach must evaluate the extent to which the skill execution matched the perfect model of the skill or task. Here the coach will also identify aspects of the skill that were performed incorrectly and establish the cause of the error. Factors affecting the error rate of a performer could be a result of primary factors connected to technique, psychological factors (e.g. low levels of confidence or high levels of anxiety), perceptual or decision-making errors, and a coach should strive to identify the root cause. At this point the coach must make a decision to either take action to remedy the situation or decide not to take any action. A coach may decide not to take any action to change the performance because of the time in the season (for example, correcting a player's shooting action prior to a competition in netball would not be feasible and should be broken down in the off-season). Following the diagnosis or analysis stage, the coach is suitably placed to begin the feedback and guidance process.

Providing Feedback

Feedback will provide the participant with knowledge, motivation and reinforcement and will often promote adherence and full commitment to the learning process. Congruent feedback maintains a focus on the learning

EFFECTIVE OBSERVATION

- Break down the action to focus on one phase, body part, coaching point or learning cue presented.
- Observe several times.
- Observe from different angles.
- Observe the outcome. (Did the participant score a goal? Did the pass reach the intended recipient?)

cues initially presented to a participant and by limiting feedback to these congruent cues ensures that the learner is not overloaded or presented with additional information not provided at the outset. Only when differentiating for an individual would the coach be expected to offer other cues. This type of feedback offers specific and qualitative information to guide the performer and is more powerful in terms of learning than the general feedback often used (for example, 'Good work'). While general comments are sometimes used for motivating or ensuring a group remain on task, they do not provide a clear focus for individuals when engaged with a learning activity.

Feedback should be positively phrased and, while there may be a need to identify what is being executed incorrectly, the coach should strive to ensure a supportive comment is provided. This is often where positive, negative and corrective components are integrated together. For example, a coach may say, 'You are trying hard, Jane, but having problems at the release point of the pass. Try extending the arm further forward and release the ball in front of the body.'

The expertise required to be successful in a coaching role is extensive. A coach must not only possess the capacity to execute the 'how to' coach skills, but also display effective interpersonal social skills. The following section looks at the characteristics of expertise required by a youth netball coach.

Characteristics of Expertise for the Youth Netball Coach

Research carried out with eleven coaches – recognized as experts in the context of youth netball coaching – identified thirty-three characteristics of expertise (Navin, 2013). These characteristics were categorized under seven themes related to sport coaching expertise (see Table 1.1).

Pedagogical knowledge is crucial when coaching children, and creating a supportive, fun and engaging climate for learning emerged as essential for this role. The importance of encouragement, praise and reinforcement to build positive relationships between coach and participant is crucial. The reason children participate in sport is to have fun, be with friends and improve technical skills. Expertise is related closely to a coach's capacity to not only break down technical skills and detect errors, but also to offer corrective measures to enhance skill development. Ensuring a session contains appropriate game-like practices and conditioned activities to promote learning would promote an authentic learning environment.

Promoting decision-making through the use of questioning and self-discovery strategies was a factor of expertise for the children's coach. The ability to ask meaningful questions is crucial when adopting a participant-centred approach.

The children's coach must have the expertise to engage in structured preparation of a session and series of coaching sessions. The need to progress skills and promote a structured and safe environment are of paramount

---

GIVING FEEDBACK

- Initially prompt the performer to engage in self-analysis.
- Give congruent feedback in a simple and supportive manner.
- Focus on only one or two key points.
- Check for understanding at the end of the dialogue with the participant.

importance in the youth context. Strachan, Côté and Deakin (2011) refer to psychological safety as a key consideration for youth sport. Psychological safety has been defined as the shared belief that the environment is appropriate for interpersonal risk-taking (Edmondson, 2003). The expert children's coach should plan appropriate progressions and coach fundamental skills in an environment where risk is minimized and physical safety has been addressed. Any coach is deemed critical in promoting and fostering positive developmental outcomes in youth sport (Fraser-Thomas, Côté and Deakin, 2005). The ability to promote the psychosocial growth of the individual through the development of confidence and self-esteem was one of the two most prominent features of expertise for the children's coach. The responsibility of the coach in this domain extends beyond that of teaching the foun-

dational skills. The coach, according to Petitpas et al. (2005), will contribute significantly to the psychosocial development of the young participants. The use of praise and reinforcement formed the second item ranked the highest in the youth coaching context.

A successful relationship within this context fosters commitment, sets appropriate boundaries and ensures the coach is approachable. For the children's coach the social (fairness, patience and approachability), emotional (inspirational) and psychological factors (commitment) are reported as critical attributes. In support of the findings, Gould and Carson (2011) outlined the need for the coach to promote the development of life skills through emphasizing hard work, being a positive role model and showing good sportsmanship. Expertise for the children's coach has rated pedagogical expertise and coach character as the most

Table 1.1   Themes associated with sport coaching expertise and the youth coach.

Theme	Overview
Wider sport knowledge	The knowledge required from outside and beyond the actual netball coaching domain
Game development	The structure of the practice environment and setting for learning
Humanistic coaching	A participant-centred approach focusing on the all-round development of the individual and where ownership of decisions is shared between coach and participant
Management and organization of the coaching process	Strategies employed by the coach in the planning, delivery and evaluation of coaching to promote a suitable environment for the participant/athlete
Coach–athlete relationship	Outlines coaching as a complex, reciprocally influential and interdependent process based on social interaction
Growth mind-set	The belief that intelligence can be developed, challenge should be embraced and mistakes are inherent in the learning process
Coach character	The attributes of the individual in the coach role

Table 1.2   Characteristics of sport coaching expertise for the youth coach in netball.

Characteristic of Expertise (n=33)	Coach Ranking
Game Development	
Uses game-like situations	19
Knowledge of corrective measures for skills	25
Can condition activities	30
Humanistic Coaching	
Will develop confidence and self-esteem	1
Promotes engagement and fun	3
Promotes decision-making	8
Promotes the involvement of everyone	13
Promotes self-reflection	13
Can personalize learning	19
Is child-centred	19
Promotes self-discovery	25
Management & Organization of the Coaching Process	
Uses praise and positive reinforcement	1
Will praise effort and success	3
Uses positive behaviour management	3
Develops rapport not friendship	3
Promotes a safe environment	8
Effective in giving instructions	13
Promotes open-ended questioning	19
Uses appropriate grouping strategies	29
Can build up skills from the basic level	25
Can progress skills at varying rates	31
Will work with a supporting coach	31
Session planning	33
Coach–Athlete Relationship	
Is approachable	13
Can set appropriate boundaries	24
Will commit time and effort	25
Coach Character	
Portrays a positive image	3
Is fair	8
Is consistent with behaviour	8
Can motivate young participants	8
Is inspirational	13
Is patient	13
Is a good leader	19

important features. The thirty-three characteristics of expertise are presented in Table 1.2.

Of notable importance and ranked highest were the factors associated with promoting and building confidence and self-esteem. The ability to praise effort and success along with the use of reinforcement was highlighted as a predominant feature of the expert characteristics of the children's coach. The ability to promote engagement and fun, develop rapport and use positive behaviour management strategies were also highly ranked. Portraying a positive image and the notion of being fair were the highest ranked characteristics within the personal qualities category of expertise.

For the children's coach the research by Navin (2013) confirmed the importance of content and pedagogical knowledge. The dual role of the coach in promoting the sport-specific development and the all-round development of the individual beyond the sport is important to note. The participation coach of children should adopt an inclusive focus (and not an exclusive selection-based approach), promote a mastery-oriented climate, ensure safety is paramount, and promote fun. Côté and Gilbert (2009) also cited the importance of teaching and assessing the development of fundamental movements in a child-centred approach and stressed the need to promote the social aspects of the sport.

CHAPTER 2

MANAGING THE YOUTH NETBALL CLUB ENVIRONMENT

Nicky Fuller

In this chapter the focus is on managing a children's netball club beyond the coaching session. It will embrace the management and sustainability of a club, and consider which key elements are necessary to make the club experience enjoyable and fulfilling for everyone involved. This will include establishing a club ethos, sound club development, working with parents, club events and managing diversity within clubs.

Involvement in a junior netball club as a coach, manager or volunteer can be one of the most rewarding of sports experiences. Achieving a well managed, supportive environment is key to a club's success and getting this right requires a well thought-out

The netball club experience should be an enjoyable experience for everyone involved.

approach. The approach should be explicit, regularly reinforced and shared by everyone involved with the club. It will form the bedrock for everything that takes place and will shape the club's image to those outside. Getting this right will make decisions associated with the club easier to make as there will be a framework to check against and processes to guide decision-making. Ensuring the ethos is understood by players, coaches, parents and volunteers alike is an ongoing part of club life.

The Club Ethos

The club ethos should underpin the approach taken by personnel working within the club. It is the most critical feature of a junior club and yet it is often the least overt part of club life. If shared and recognized it ensures that everyone is singing the same tune and can avoid potential embarrassments that sometimes come to light in the media. An example of misunderstanding ethos in a junior football club resulted in national media coverage when a coach sent parents of his U10 football squad an email saying:

'I am not there so the boys can have fun playing football – I am only interested in winning.' He went on: 'I don't care about equal play time or any other communist view of sport... life will be competitive, so get them used to it.' (*Daily Mail*, Inderdeep Bains and Ray Massey, 3 December 2013.)

When parents complained to the club and one parent sent the content of the email to the *Daily Mail*, the club were quick to respond saying, 'This is a friendly village football club that just wants to get as many children playing football as possible, and make sure they have fun doing it.'

Had the club made their values clear from the outset and used it when recruiting coaches, it may have avoided national news

and the coach is unlikely to have joined the club given his strong views on children's sport. While this case may appear obtuse, many clubs face challenges when volunteers or parents have views misaligned with those of the club. In these instances it is important that someone from the club discusses the situation with the person involved before it escalates.

Developing the ethos should involve all club personnel – coaches, volunteers, officials,

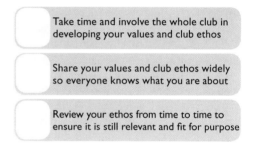

Fig. 2.1   The club ethos.

committee members – and then be refined through discussion and consultation. This may take some time and involve changes; however, if it is going to work for the club and have buy-in from everyone involved, it is worth being patient and developing an ethos that is unique to the club and genuinely agreed by everyone involved. The following are some typical examples of club ethos:

- The primary aim of our club is to provide playing opportunities for all within the local community.
- The club is dedicated to the growth of netball and to providing structured coaching for the development of young players, on which the game and club depend for sustained growth.
- All players have the right to play netball at the highest standard they are capable of,

All volunteers in a club should share the values of the club ethos and be committed to it.

so that the game is both challenging and competitive, with the overall aim of enjoyment of the sport in a safe environment.

- The club is committed to maintaining its reputation as an actively social club, being inclusive not exclusive, where young people come to play and socialize in equal measure and where elite netball is just one element and not the overriding consideration.
- Individual and team success is encouraged and strived for, but not to the detriment of the key values of player enjoyment and equality of opportunity.
- Our netball club provides an environment in which every player is valued for their own abilities and where we will promote fair play and a place for all players to experience personal success, fun and team spirit.

It would be very easy to extract and copy part of an ethos from other clubs. However, the process of developing your own club ethos should prompt thinking about how you will meet the values and sentiments that the club aspires to. It will also be important to ensure that the philosophy of coaches, the codes of conduct for players, officials and parents are all congruent with the overall ethos of the club. The ethos gives you an opportunity to build an inspirational and aspirational picture for children's netball and raise the profile of the club.

Sharing the club ethos is important for existing and new club members as well as potential partners such as local schools, sports development organizations, your governing body at local/regional level and sponsors. The ethos can be promoted through internal meetings, club inductions and recruitment, posters, the website, through talks with parents and at club presentations. Once you have shared it, the challenge will be to live up to the values you have identified and to use it as a guide for decision-making within the club, particularly around ethical and conduct-related decisions.

For example, if as a club you claim to 'be open to all' you need to work to ensure you truly are. Barriers such as costs and how you structure the payment of club fees and kit purchases will be important. Upfront, lump sum payment of annual fees and kit costs will exclude some potential young members whose families struggle to make such payments. If you are really 'open to all' you will have procedures in place for different payment methods and reduced rates for those children who are eligible for free school meals. Likewise the cost of kit should be considered so that it is affordable.

Careful consideration needs to be given regarding what the club can resource. It might not be possible to offer training and competitive opportunities for players of *all* abilities and there is no shame in that. Rather, the shame would be in not recognizing that the

Every player should be valued and supported in their development.

club is unable to meet the needs of all players, resulting in children having negative experiences of sports clubs and the game of netball. The size of the club and its catchment might determine the strength of squads and the level of competition available. Having an ethos where the club feeds more talented players onto clubs playing in higher level leagues or with a stronger performance section demonstrates player centredness and that the club has players' best interests at the heart of what it does. The same can be said of clubs who clearly signpost players whose needs as a recreational or social player cannot be met within the club. The key thing is that clubs recognize individual needs and have strong links with partner organizations that are able to complement their own resources. Working together with feeder schools, neighbour-

ing clubs and other organizations that provide fluid opportunities for young players to move in and across clubs demonstrates a mature approach to meeting the needs of individuals. After all, we don't expect children to stay in infant school for their entire education; we expect them to move to different schools and work in different groups according to their needs.

In recognizing that netball clubs can and do have a positive and profound impact on young people's lives comes the responsibility to create positive choices towards involvement in physical activity and healthy lifestyles. It is generally acknowledged that early experiences of sport greatly influence an individual's future involvement and engagement. For clubs aiming to grow the game, it is important for them to make the early experiences of the game and the netball club positive. It has long been recognized (Lerner, 2005) that positive sports coaching experiences support young people way beyond the court through building social networks, growing self-esteem and self-confidence, creating connections with sport and healthy lifestyles.

Côté and Gilbert (2009) have developed a widely acknowledged model that seeks to maximize the gains traditionally linked to sports coaching and use them to drive personal and social development of young performers. Known as the 'C', the model focuses on the development of the 'whole child'. While this has been promoted in coaching, it is really the responsibility of the whole club to drive the philosophy approach of the 'C' system; it should not be left to the coaching staff alone. The Cs that are recognized as core to personal and social development are:

Competence: Developing and recognizing technical, tactical, physical and mental capabilities that emerge through appropriate activities, enabling personal development and success.

Confidence: This is a critical area of personal development that clubs can be proud to support: establishing a culture through the club that enables children to experience success through individual and group challenges as well as helping to develop strategies to build resilience and manage failure. This

is achieved through valuing effort, improvement and persistence rather than results and outcomes.

Connection: Helping players to love the game and love the sport. It is about building connections with other players, coaches and volunteers in the club.

Character and Caring: Developing a strong respect for fair play, rules and appropriate behaviours for the sport. It is also about developing respect for self, the club, facilities and equipment and other players (team and opposition). Helping children to take responsibility for their own behaviour is key to this.

Creativity: Enabling young people to work out solutions for themselves. Netball is a sport that is well placed for this as players need to think about how to find ways of beating an opponent – working with team-mates, finding spaces in small areas, and so on. It is not developed by players following set patterns and only responding to instructions.

The five Cs listed here are developed as much off the court as they are on the court. Team managers, officials and volunteers are all able to play a role in developing the whole child through careful planning and being mindful of the importance of these five social and personal development areas.

It is always interesting to ask club person-

> Ensure the club has clear governance through a constitution

> Make sure you have defined roles for your Management Committee – this will make recruitment and on-going management smooth

> Ensure you have key policies and procedures that are current and fit for purpose

Fig.2.2   Key points for the structure of the club.

nel to rate the club's success at the end of a season. It gives an indication of how they measure the club's success, for example by competitive outcomes, numbers of players reaching talent squads, number of new players recruited, satisfaction ratings, number of new volunteers, etc. If the central success rating is out of kilter with the club's ethos then it tells you that the ethos needs reinforcing!

Reviewing your club ethos at appropriate times – usually biennially or every three years – will ensure that it reflects contemporary thinking for a modern sports club. It will also allow you to change and amend it as the club continually develops.

Club Management and Administration

Having sound and transparent decision-making routes helps with effective club management. Making it clear to everyone who makes the decisions and how to do so within the club should be through appropriate routes such as a club committee. Most netball governing bodies in the UK have schemes that either accredit or recommend good club management processes and systems. Getting the mechanics of committee meetings, constitutions, rules and policies clarified and in place will help the club run smoothly.

Constitution

Every club should have a constitution, as it sets out the purpose and rules of your sports club. It is the key document that will ensure smooth and proper running of club affairs. Typically, the constitution will set out:

- The objectives for your club (e.g. what you want to do or provide for everyone involved).
- Different forms of membership (e.g. U11,

U14, U16, coach, volunteer) and perhaps their subscription rates.
- The rules which your club will operate by.
- How the club will be managed (e.g. by officers and a committee).
- How the members input to the club management, usually through an annual general meeting.

It is highly recommended that junior netball clubs, once established and operating, adopt a constitution. A copy of a sample constitution can be found at the end of this chapter. Beware that not all the elements in the sample constitution will be relevant to every club and they should be amended or deleted as appropriate. For example, your club's constitution may need to reduce or increase the number or range of 'officers', depending on the number of volunteers available to fill the positions.

Meetings

Clubs require a structure in which to organize their meetings. The rules for meetings should be referred to in the constitution (e.g. the quorum).

Committee meetings are organized by the elected officers in order to manage the day-to-day running of the club. Regular meetings ensure that the club is successfully planning, communicating and monitoring progress. It is vital to make sure that these meetings are kept short and to the point, and that they are completely necessary, otherwise there is a danger of putting people off taking a role in the club. It is useful to set out guidelines for the conduct of committee meetings. This might include: length of meeting, number of meetings per year, number of days notice, sending out of papers beforehand.

The role of the officers on the club's Management Committee vary from club to club, depending on the sport and the size or level

Volunteers will support the day-to-day running of the netball club.

of the club. Some clubs only need to have one Management Committee while other larger clubs may have a series of sub- committees – a playing and competition committee, a development committee or a finance committee – which feed into a main or executive committee.

There are many varied roles and workloads taken on by officers on management committees. It is important to avoid having the same few officers take on all the officer roles and doing the majority of the work. Having a clear role description for each role is very important when recruiting new volunteers within your club; at the end of this chapter you will find some role descriptions for key committee officers.

Programmes such as 'Club Leaders' developed through Sport England provide free support for club officers, with online resources, face-to-face workshops and mentoring. The topics cover business and financial planning, marketing, governance and facility manage-ment. The website can be found at www. sportenglandclubleaders.com.

Policies and Procedures

As your sports club grows and develops, you may find it necessary to establish some club policies that set out in more detail how the club and its members should operate. The range of policies and procedures that might be required will very much depend on the nature of your club and the range of activities that you organize. The following gives an outline of typical policies held by a netball club.

Membership policy: membership criteria and membership forms.

Equity policy: establishing an equity statement and its implementation.

Code of conduct for players, volunteers, coaches, parents: this includes a different code of conduct for each of the above and identifies the expected standards of participation and play.

Safeguarding young people, including guidance on the use of social media: procedures to safeguard children and young people participating in the club's activities. See your respective governing body website for the most current version of its recommended safeguarding policy for junior players in your country.

Health and safety: covering a range of issues including duty of care, risk assessment, insurance, first aid, emergency procedures, etc.

Use of social networking within the club: guidance on how social networking should be managed and used by members of the club for club-based communication.

A range of examples of these policies and guidance notes can be found on netball governing body websites. In addition, the 'Clubmark' website is aimed at minimum standards for junior sports clubs and has a range of template policies and procedures that would be suitable for junior netball clubs to use. The site can be found at www.clubmark.org.uk/what-clubmark.

Noting an individual's age and stage of development must be considered when planning a netball programme. For example, for a player who is under eleven, a netball session should last between 60 and 90 minutes.

Club Insurance

Insurance – club insurance as opposed to individual coach insurance or umpire insurance – is a very important responsibility for all clubs. It is important to check that insurance adequately covers your club for the activities it delivers, i.e. competition, training, travel to tournaments and overnight stays. Club insurance is usually secured through club affiliation with the national governing body. If your governing body does not offer insurance it is highly recommended that this is sought through a reputable insurance broker who will cover all members of the club and all club activities.

Working with Parents and Carers

Netball, like other sports, faces the dilemma of striking the right balance when it comes to parental involvement. Parents are an integral part of the sporting landscape for young people – after all, they provide transport, supply nutrition, are key in motivating and encouraging their children, make sure they get the right amount of sleep and try to achieve balance with schoolwork and other sports, etc. However, some young players find parents embarrassing to be around, and some players demonstrate different behaviour if their parents are present. Likewise, parents' enthusiasm can become over-ambitious and in a minority of cases clubs would prefer some parents to stay well away!

Nevertheless, it is important to make parents feel welcome and share what you expect from them early on, so that they are aware of the club's standards and ethos for young people. Issuing a simple code of conduct for parents and carers when a child joins the club encourages parental support but identifies the boundaries of acceptable behaviour, and potential sanctions should these be breached.

A sample code of conduct for parents/carers is provided at the end of this chapter. It should be stressed that simply issuing the code of conduct will not be the panacea for all issues regarding parents. Communicating and regularly working with parents in sharing the decision-making around areas that may create tensions, such as team selections or squad changes, will help in managing potential problems. Holding parent events where information can be exchanged around the development of the young athlete helps to keep parents on board and aware of the position of the club and its coaches and volunteers. Parents and carers can often be converted into volunteers and take on roles within the club if they are made to feel welcome.

Managing Diversity

Creating a vibrant, safe and progressive club that embraces players from all communities will help the club to grow and sustain the next generation of club members. To do this well clubs should engage with and understand who its current members are and where they are from. It should also demonstrate an awareness and appreciation of its local community and encourage new members from that community. Checking how well you are doing in this can be gauged through a number of methods, including an annual audit of club members, exit questionnaires, and anonymous feedback within the club from players, coaches, volunteers and parents. It's an open and healthy way to reflect and move forward.

Training and Competition Structure

Traditionally, junior netball clubs organize their training around age groups (U11, U14, U16), which often reflects the competition structure that teams will be entering. While this is pragmatic for entering competitions and managing new cohorts of players, it is not necessarily player-centred and coaches should be encouraged to look at long-term athlete development models when selecting players to squads. This takes into account training age, developmental age (physical and mental) and performance ability when grouping players, rather than age alone. It will allow flexibility to move players across squads according to needs, rather than being restricted to age alone. However, if entering competitions it is important that players are not too old to play within an age group category.

Put the young person at the heart of decisions when selecting squads and entering competitions

Ensure all competitions and training are suitable for the ability and development of players

Ensure training is an enjoyable experience for all players involved – creating strong early connections is vital for a life in sport and netball

Fig. 2.3   Policies and procedures.

When planning training sessions the club, in conjunction with coaches, needs to consider a number of factors, including:

How long? As a rule of thumb, players aged twelve to eighteen should train no longer than 2 hours at a time – particularly during school term time, while they are in education. So a training session may range from 1 hour through to 2 hours. For under eleven age groups 90 minutes is possibly the maximum timeframe for training to maintain the level of concentration and physical effort required during a session. However, there are times when a training session may be much longer than this, for example, during training camps or holiday sessions. These tend to be one-off sessions held during holiday times and have a different focus to regular training sessions.

How often and when should clubs train? This may depend on the availability of coaches and volunteers and venue availability. It can vary from twice weekly through to monthly and anything in between, depending on squads, their goals and the focus of the club. Clearly the more regularly players train, the greater improvements they are likely to make with good coaching. However, consideration should also be given to other netball training that players might be receiving at school, area/representative level, etc. For many junior clubs weekly or fortnightly sessions would tend to be the norm. In terms of when training

should take place, this again may be influenced by availability of personnel and venues. However, there are certain times that should be avoided, such as later evenings. The younger the player, the earlier the training should be or else it could be held on a weekend day. If players have to travel for some time to reach the club, this should also be considered when setting finishing times. Young people – particularly those involved with intense physical activity – need sleep. Late nights should not be demanded by netball training sessions. Working back from a reasonable bedtime, the club should consider that young people may need to travel, eat and bath/shower following training and possibly complete homework.

How many weeks over the year? Ideally, clubs should try to break their year down into blocks of time so that they can structure their training across the year. This is often termed 'periodization' and in its simplest form means that you would have certain periods of training with a certain focus, as follows:

General preparation phase – the focus in this phase is fitness and basic or individual technical skills, with some work on unit and team play moving into the competition phase. It is a good timeframe to work on specialist skills such as shooting.

Competition phase – the focus in this phase is about maintaining levels of fitness

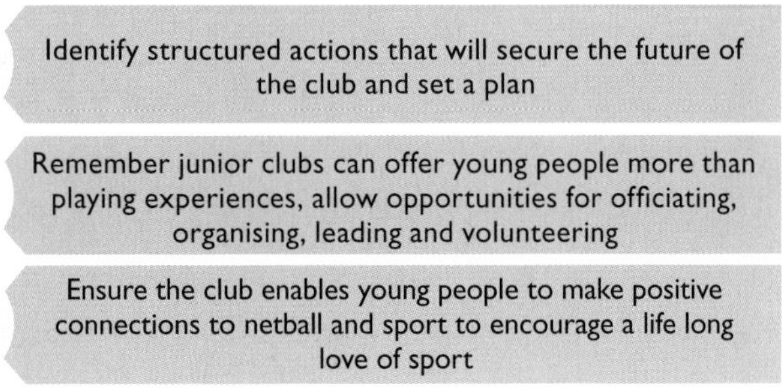

Identify structured actions that will secure the future of the club and set a plan

Remember junior clubs can offer young people more than playing experiences, allow opportunities for officiating, organising, leading and volunteering

Ensure the club enables young people to make positive connections to netball and sport to encourage a life long love of sport

Fig. 2.4   Look to the future in your planning – for the club as well as individuals.

and preparing for matches. With junior players this is still likely to involve development of technical skills but will have a greater focus on tactical play than the previous phases.

Transition phase – in this phase the focus is on recovery and physical and mental regeneration. It is helpful to have a complete break from netball, although players should be encouraged to maintain a basic level of fitness by enjoying other sports.

During the management of training and competition programmes it is critical that young players are at the heart of any decision-making. Young players are often involved in training/competitions (school, club, local league, possibly a representative squad) as well as being involved in other sports or other pursuits such as music or drama. One way of ensuring balance in a young player's life and not being over-demanding is by encouraging each player to have a Child Athlete Management Plan (CHAMP) – this is simply a weekly diary that outlines training/competition/other pursuits, etc. It need not be required by all club players, but is extremely useful for those with lots of commitments in their life and is something that will help club coaches, the player and their parents begin to identify bottlenecks and plan and make decisions about which areas should be given priority.

Additional Club Playing Activities

In addition to regular training sessions the club might consider some of the following activities:

Summer/holiday training camps – these can be fun for young people as they give them time to immerse themselves in the sport in a fun environment. They have the additional benefit of enabling connections to be developed with netball, other players, coaches and the club. Spending a longer time on skills can help children build confidence and new skills. These sessions can be a good recruitment tool too if they are open to any player or non-members. The camps can also be a great place for young coaches and umpires to help out.

Specialist training sessions – sometimes regular training sessions do not afford the time to give specialist input for specific skills. Setting up sessions outside regular training sessions can allow the club to support players on specific skills. These might include the following: shooting, skills for circle defence, personal goal setting, specific fitness training, etc.

Weekend tournaments and competitions with overnight stays – there are a number of companies and organizations that specialize in setting up junior netball tournaments, usually held in ready-made holiday camps. These events can be good for team-building and help to really develop skills off the court between players as well as providing a full competition schedule. Clubs need to be well prepared and aware of safeguarding issues when taking groups away. Guidance for this sort of activity can be found with the national governing body.

Non-Playing Club Activities

For young people a netball club can provide opportunities beyond playing, such as trying out **leadership roles**. These might include courses for young umpires and young leaders/coaches, either hosted at the club or identified through local contacts. Some governing bodies have schemes for young volunteers that recognize their role and offer rewards after a number of hours of volunteering. For example, England Netball has such a scheme called 'Pass on your Passion', which can be accessed by junior members.

Awards night and celebrations are important in recognizing efforts and successes in the club. Such events can be a way of celebrating the club's achievements beyond playing too – identifying efforts and contributions of young players off the court, such as helping out with younger players or umpiring. Awards need to be carefully thought out and effort can be rewarded alongside recognition of great performances. Such events also provide another opportunity to bring in parents so that they are able to recognize the work of the club and some of its broader achievements that go beyond 'best player'. Getting all players to recognize the contributions that another player makes at the club is a potential way of ensuring all players are recognized.

Planning and Development

In busy junior clubs, day-to-day operation and management sometimes takes over and leaves little time for planning and thinking about longer term priorities and developments. However, for the future of the club it is essential to have at least an annual plan so that everyone knows what is to be completed and developed, and by when. Typically a netball club development/action plan would cover issues such as:

- coaching (recruitment, training courses, qualifications)
- umpiring/officiating (recruitment, training, qualifications)
- equipment/venue (purchases, renewal, expansion)
- player recruitment (numbers, age groups, school links)
- volunteers (areas of need, recruitment, training)

- management (fundraising, marketing, promotion)
- playing opportunities (league entries, age group development)

Within each of these areas the club should scope out:

- specific action/s and what needs to be done
- who will lead on the action and ensure its completion
- the timescale – usually when the action will be completed
- costs and resources

This need not be a long document; a page of A4 may be sufficient for a small club while others may require a longer document depending on aspirations. Remember, a club that stands still and does not develop is in fact going backwards!

Guidance for the Use of Social Networking Sites

The use of social media is extensive by most young people and is often their preferred means of communication and receiving information. Social media is a useful and important tool which helps with instant communication and promotion at low cost. It is, however, important to make sure safeguards are put into place to protect users from harm as well as protecting the club and club personnel.

The following guidance is aimed at protecting users and preventing allegations and issues arising from the use of social media:

Make sure you know how to operate the social media that you use: For example, if you have chosen to use Twitter, make sure you understand how it operates, and how to set privacy or a 'closed' access to invited members; check what safeguards are already in place and how you can use them.

Building connections with other individuals in the club is encouraged.

Manage your social media: Nominate a responsible adult to manage the site and content. This person will need to be trained in how to spot the warning signs of bullying, inappropriate content posted, etc. They should also be required to complete a DBS check. Regular monitoring is required to control comments and photo uploads and remove any that are inappropriate or may cause offence to other users. If the site allows it, make sure no material can be published without the manager checking it first. Do not ask for personal contact details from users, especially young people; this includes their location and school or other information that may put them at risk.

Target the right age group: Make sure the content of the site is relevant to the age group you are targeting. No illegal, inappropriate or adult content should be allowed. Do not target children under the age that may be restricted for the site, e.g. for Facebook those under the age of thirteen.

Promote safety: Make sure users know how to protect themselves online and promote websites where they can receive support and advice, such as www.ceop.police.uk and www.thinkuknow.co.uk.

Personal details: Do not ask users for personal or contact details, including their school, college or location.

For coaches/volunteers using social media within the club:

- Separate personal and professional social networking identities by setting up a separate account when communicating with junior members.
- Remember that any photos, video clips and comments uploaded to the internet may be there forever, even if you delete them, and may be viewed by people who you may not think will see them. Make sure they are appropriate for everyone to view and adhere to the club's policy.
- Choose a profile picture with care.
- Do not give out personal details such as your address, mobile number or location on any website unless you have separate professional contact details.
- Make sure your personal social networking profile is set to private or for friends only.
- If you communicate with players under the age of eighteen make sure you have permission to do so from parents/carers. Always copy another colleague or welfare officer into the message/communication.

SAMPLE CONSTITUTION

I Name
The club will be called xxxxxxx and will be affiliated to [name of country governing body, e.g. England Netball].

2 Aims and objectives
The aims and objectives of the club will be:

* to offer coaching and competitive opportunities in netball to junior players aged x–x years
* to promote the club within [name of local area] and surrounding areas through primary and secondary schools, and other relevant organizations
* to ensure a duty of care to all members of the club
* to ensure that present and future members all have access to fair and equal treatment.

3 Membership
Membership should consist of officers and members of the club. Membership of the club is through completion of the club membership consent form (and payment of membership fees).

Membership fees will be set annually and agreed by the Management Committee or determined at the Annual General Meeting.

4 Officers of the club
The officers of the club will be:

* Chair
* Honorary Secretary
* Treasurer
* Fixtures Secretary
* Publicity Officer
* Team Manager
* Coach representative
* Player representative
* Club Welfare Officer

Officers will be elected annually at the Annual General Meeting.

All officers will retire each year but will be eligible for re-appointment.

5 Committee
The club will be managed through the Management Committee consisting of: Chair, Honorary Secretary, Treasurer, Fixtures Secretary, Publicity Officer, Team Manager, Club Welfare Officer and Coach representative and Player representative. Only these posts will have the right to vote at meetings of the Management Committee.

The Management Committee will be convened by the Secretary of the club and held no less than twice per year.

The quorum required for business to be agreed at Management Committee meetings will be: four.

The Management Committee will be responsible for adopting new policy, codes of conduct and rules that affect the organization of the club.

The Management Committee will have powers to appoint sub-committees as necessary and appoint advisers to the Management Committee as necessary to fulfill its business.

The Management Committee will be responsible for setting up disciplinary hearings of members who infringe the club rules/regulations/constitution. The Management Committee will be responsible for taking any action of suspension or discipline following such hearings.

6 Finance

All club monies will be banked in an account held in the name of the club.

The Club Treasurer will be responsible for the finances of the club.

The financial year of the club will end on: [month]

A statement of annual accounts will be presented by the Treasurer at the Annual General Meeting.

7 Annual General Meetings

Notice of the Annual General Meeting (AGM) will be given by the Club Secretary. Not less than 21 clear days' notice to be given to all members.

The AGM will receive a report from officers of the Management Committee and a statement of the accounts.

Nominations for officers of the Management Committee can be sent to the Secretary prior to the AGM or made at the meeting.

Elections of officers are to take place at the AGM.

All members have the right to vote at the AGM.

The quorum for AGMs will be [10%] of the membership.

The Management Committee has the right to call Extraordinary General Meetings (EGMs) outside the AGM. Procedures for EGMs will be the same as for the AGM.

8 Discipline and appeals

All complaints regarding the behaviour of members should be submitted in writing to the Secretary.

The Management Committee will set up a group to hear complaints within fourteen days of a complaint being lodged. The committee has the power to take appropriate disciplinary action, including the termination of membership.

The outcome of a disciplinary hearing should be notified in writing to the person who lodged the complaint and the member against whom the complaint was made within seven days of the hearing.

There will be the right of appeal to the Management Committee following disciplinary action being announced. The committee should consider the appeal within fourteen days of the Secretary receiving the appeal.

9   Dissolution
A resolution to dissolve the club can only be passed at an AGM or EGM through a majority vote of the membership.

In the event of dissolution, any assets of the club that remain will become the property of another club with similar objectives to the club – this should be decided at the AGM/EGM.

10   Amendments to the constitution
The constitution will only be changed through agreement by majority vote at an AGM or EGM.

11   Declaration
[Name of club] hereby adopts and accepts this constitution as a current operating guide regulating the actions of members.

SIGNED: DATE:

Name:

Club Chair

SIGNED: DATE:

Name:

Club Secretary

NETBALL CLUB: ROLE DESCRIPTIONS

The following outlines the roles and responsibilities of key Committee members of the club.

Chairperson

The Chair shall:

- Be responsible for the Committee meetings and for managing the affairs of the club.
- Take the chair at Committee meetings.
- Liaise with the Secretary on the Agenda items for each meeting and approve the minutes prior to circulation.
- Be familiar with the constitution of the Club and with the mission statement, visions and objectives of the club and England Netball.
- Support and where necessary co-ordinate the work of other committee members.
- Be responsible, in conjunction with the Secretary and Treasurer, for the presentation of the Annual Report.
- Delegate areas of meeting to the Vice Chair when and where appropriate.
- If unavailable to attend a meeting, brief the Vice-Chair on the Agenda of that meeting.
- Ensure the Club adheres to the England Netball Duty of Care guidelines.

Vice Chairperson

The Vice Chairperson shall:

- Take the chair at Committee meetings when the Chairperson is unable to attend and at a time when the Chairperson wishes to take part in discussion.
- Support the Chair in planning agendas and take responsibility for areas delegated by the Chair.
- Ensure the Club adheres to all policies agreed regarding the club's operation and management.

Secretary

The Secretary shall:

- Liaise with the Chair on the Agenda and Minutes for each meeting prior to them being circulated.
- Take minutes at all Committee meetings and Annual General Meetings.
- Send a letter to all players and volunteers giving notice of the AGM and the relevant information associated with the AGM.
- Prepare the Annual Report to be submitted at the AGM.
- Circulate any relevant information received from league/county/region and other partners/ organizations.
- Circulate any other relevant information as appropriate within timelines.
- Ensure the club adheres to England Netball Duty of Care guidelines.

Treasurer

The Treasurer shall:

- Be responsible for the management of the club's finances in accordance with the decisions of the Committee and have the right to query any expenditure.
- Recommend action on financial matters to the committee.
- Ensure that all payments are made by the date requested.
- Present written financial reports to meetings of the Committee.
- Present an Annual report at the Committee's AGM.

- Be responsible for all monies belonging to the club.
- Ensure due diligence to all expenditure, investments and income.

Kit Manager

The Kit Manager shall:
- Be responsible for allocating and collecting match kit at appropriate times during the season.
- Keep an audit of kit owned and held by the club.
- Identify when new kit is required and make orders for kit when agreed by Treasurer and Committee.
- Order sundry kit required by players (hoodies/knickers/tracksuit bottoms).

Publicity Officer

The Publicity Officer shall:
- Be responsible for promoting the club and informing press and other organizations of the club's successes.
- Putting reports into local press.
- Ensure that the club adheres to England Netball Safeguarding guidelines for all publicity work.
- Liaise with the website manager to ensure current news on the website.

Coaches

Coaches shall:
- Attend training sessions as agreed by the club.
- Plan training sessions relevant to the age and stage of development.
- Coach all players to the best of their ability.
- Give due diligence to safety of all players at all times.
- Focus on coaching the player rather than the game.
- Keep personal standards high through adopting the coach's code of conduct.
- Ensure coaching practice is current and up to date.
- Ensure that coaching practice adheres to England Netball Safeguarding guidelines for all publicity work.

Umpires

Umpires shall:
- Represent the club where umpires are required.
- Attend training sessions to practise and to support player development where required.
- Keep personal standards high through adopting the official code of conduct.
- Ensure umpiring practice is current and up to date.
- Ensure that the umpiring practice adheres to England Netball Safeguarding guidelines for all publicity work.

Volunteer Coordinator

The Volunteer Coordinator shall:
- Be the main point of contact for volunteers and volunteering within the club.
- Identify the volunteer needs of the club.
- Recruit new volunteers.
- Screen new volunteers.
- Ensure that volunteers receive appropriate feedback and support.
- Ensure that the club has systems to recognize and reward volunteer contribution.
- Link to local volunteering programmes and initiatives.

CODE OF CONDUCT FOR PARENTS, CARERS AND SUPPORTERS

As a parent, carer and supporter of xxxx Netball Club, the club encourages your support of players and your own child. We want to encourage you to do this in a way that will most benefit all involved. The following guidelines are aimed at helping everyone to enjoy netball.

- Do not force an unwilling child to participate in netball.
- Remember children are involved in netball for their enjoyment, not yours.
- Encourage your children to play to the rules and not to argue with umpires or other officials.
- Teach your child that honest effort is more important than victory so that the result of each game is accepted without undue disappointment.
- Turn losing into winning by helping your child work towards skill improvement and good sportsmanship.
- Never ridicule or yell at a child for making a mistake or losing a game.
- Remember that children learn best by example. Applaud good play by your team and by members of the opposition.
- Do not question the umpire's decisions or honesty. Remember he/she is only human with the same feelings as you, and like you, can sometimes make an honest error.
- Recognize the importance and value of coaches who are all volunteers. They give children their time and resources to provide netball for your child.
- Remember coaches are often tied up with planning and organization before the start and at the very end of a session. If you need to chat to them about your child please approach the coach at a convenient time that does not take them away from their role of coaching the children.
- Read the rules of netball to understand better what you are watching and commenting on.
- Promote this code of conduct to other parents, carers and supporters.

CHAPTER 3

PLANNING A YOUTH NETBALL SESSION

Anita Navin

A successful coaching session needs to be planned and will relate closely to the overall annual plan. It goes without saying that those coaches who fail to plan will undoubtedly plan to fail. The coach must always adopt a player-centred approach and in doing this ensure that the needs of the participants are put first rather than the activity, parents, coach goals or ambitions. Each individual (regardless of age, ability or disability) in a session must be viewed as someone with unique needs, interests and goals. A coach who possesses the knowledge of how a session should be structured will be able to deliver a session that contains appropriate progression and ultimately achieves its purpose.

THE CONTENT OF A SESSION

- introduction and warm-up
- a skill development section
- a competitive element (small sided or full game)
- a cool-down and conclusion

The session plan outline assists the coach in structuring and designing a session and it is recommended that all coaches complete one of these for each session delivered.

A Step-by-Step Guide to Session Planning

When planning a session the following aspects should be considered and documented.

Session Goals

It is essential that the coach states clearly what the participants should be able to do by the end of a session and that the intentions are marked as session goals on the plan. There should not be too many goals to achieve and the goals must be measurable – for example, to be able to execute a shoulder pass at the appropriate time.

A coach should use the SMART acronym to ensure that the goals set are accurate. All goals should be:

Specific   For example, use a change of direction to get free at the appropriate time.

Measurable For example, always look to pass forwards for the first option.

Adjustable Through monitoring of progress the goal may not be achievable, meaning the coach has to make adjustments.

Realistic   A goal should be challenging but within the reach of a performer.

Time-based Goals should be set for the session (short term) and they should link closely to the intermediate and long-term goals for the participants.

Coaches should also set personal goals for the session that relate to their own coaching skills and performance. These personal goals allow coaches to continue their professional development by continually reviewing their performance.

Equipment

A coach should know what equipment is available in order to plan for the session and this should be appropriate for the group. For example, U11 participants will use a size 4 ball as opposed to size 5.

Duration

It is vital that in the planning stages the coach is aware of the duration of the session. The length of a session should take account of

TOP TIPS FOR THE WARM-UP

- Start slowly and gradually increase the intensity.
- Activities should be relevant to the focus of the skill section.
- Include dynamic mobility not static stretching.
- Vary the activities and make them fun.

the playing level and stage of development of the individuals – for example, a 90-minute session should be the maximum time for a potential player, whereas an open age group player will often train for a 2-hour period. In the planning stage a coach should ensure that the time is maximized by planning smooth transitions from one activity to another. Once the content of the session has been decided the coach should allocate

A warm-up will prepare the individual both physically and psychologically for the session ahead.

a period of time to each phase of the session, acknowledging the transition time between activities.

Number of Participants

A coach should know how many participants will be at the session and also give consideration to the different ability levels, development and training ages. Any individual medical or health issues should also be considered in light of the content.

Content
Warm-up

The warm-up should prepare participants mentally and physically for the subsequent activities by incorporating dynamic mobility activities and ball work.

The following dynamic movement activities are examples of what should feature in the early stages of the warm-up. Once completed, the sport-specific work can begin.

Examples:

- Side-stepping, leading with the right and left leg.
- Skipping with a low knee lift.
- Skipping with a high knee lift, adding arm swings.
- Stretching the calf muscle in the lunge position and simultaneously swinging one arm in a spiral pattern, repeating on the other leg.
- Carioca stepping followed by wide leg squats (lead left then right leg).
- Lunging forwards in a variety of directions and simultaneously reaching arms into various directions.
- Ankle rolls for 10 metres, heel flicks for 10 metres, ankle rolls followed by a two-footed jump.
- Falling start, then sprint forward with three quick steps and repeat.

- Hamstring stretch in standing position while turning trunk to either side. Repeat with the other leg.
- Sprint forwards for five strides, stop, return backwards with diagonal stepovers to the right. Repeat but then diagonally back to the left. Repeat to complete three in each direction.

Considerations for content in session planning

There are several factors which could impact upon the content of a session – for example, the stage in the season, previous performances in competition and training, lifestyle issues and player motivation. A coach should select the practices, progressions and game activities required to achieve the session goals. Progressions should be carefully planned to ensure an appropriate increase in complexity. All progressions should begin in a closed practice situation (i.e. no defenders, limited movement and a small number of participants) and gradually increase in terms of complexity, pressure situations and level of decision-making expected from the participants in the practice.

It is also important to be able to adapt

PROGRESSIONS FOR PASSING PRACTICES

- Static participants
- Participants on the move
- Increase the number of participants for passing options
- Add direction to the practice (moving to goal)
- Reduce the space available
- Add defenders (passive – active)
- Set play situations (centre pass, side line throw-in, etc.)
- Small sided game

Passing practices should always include a game-like context.

any practice planned should the number of participants change, for example when planning for an even number but one player does not attend the session. Some participants may find a practice too easy or too difficult compared to others and so alternative tasks or targets will need to be planned if this happens.

For each practice the coach should ensure that one or two coaching points are stated on the session plan to ensure that the participants have clear points to focus on in order to improve their performance.

Adapting an activity

Activities will need to be adapted to suit all individuals within a session as there may be individual differences related to ability, experience, developmental level, physiological aspects and attention span.

Tips for adapting an activity:

- Modify equipment, e.g. use a smaller ball.
- Adapt the rules – e.g. a player may hold the ball for 4 seconds in the game – to ensure certain skills are practised.
- Modify the practice by making the area smaller if the practice focus is on getting free from an opponent, or increase the area if the practice has a defending focus. Increasing the number of participants in a practice means the ball carrier has more decisions to make.
- Individuals with special needs must not be neglected and participants with visual impairments will require a coach to use their name more frequently. Using a ball with a bell inside is a useful aid. Individuals with speech or hearing impairments will need more time to convey their thoughts

and the coach should use visual cues where possible. For example, the official may have a flag to raise if the whistle cannot be heard when an infringement has occurred.

Volume and intensity

A coach must ensure that there are a sufficient number of hydration breaks within the session and also ensure that participants have appropriate work-to-rest ratios. If a practice involves sprinting (for example, sprinting to receive a pass over 10 metres) a player must ensure that the appropriate work rate is maintained, otherwise the practice effect cannot be achieved. When working on a practice involving short sprints, an individual on average will be able to complete between six and eight repetitions before performance levels deteriorate. This period of work should be followed by a rest period, giving time for the body to recover (work to rest = 1:2 or 1:3 depending on fitness levels).

Task and Group Management

When planning the session a coach must ensure that all space is used effectively and groups have clear boundaries within which they can practise. The session plan should identify the areas within which the groups will work and often a coach will use court markings in a sports hall or cones to communicate the working areas to the group.

Grouping is also a key consideration when planning; a coach can group according to ability, friendship, developmental level or randomly. Ensuring that individuals are challenged in the group activities is a paramount concern and so ability groupings may be more beneficial. A coach should vary the groupings within and between sessions to ensure that individuals are able to work with a range of individuals as the season progresses.

The session plan should contain brief information and if required a diagram to show how many individuals are in a group and the allocated working space. Any coach should plan

Grouping is important – a coach should vary who works with who in order to promote an individual's social development.

for fewer or more participants by planning practices, which can be adapted for different numbers. The timings for each task should be noted in the appropriate column in order to guide the coach and these should be evaluated on completion of a session.

Coaching Points

The coaching point column of a session plan will contain the one or two key points for the learning activity. The coaching points listed here will be the key points the coach identifies when presenting the activity or skill and they will form the basis of all observations carried out by the coach. The information will guide the analysis carried out in the session by the coach and serve to remind the coach of the components of effective performance.

Participants should always hydrate in the cool-down.

Coaches may also list the types of questions they may ask at various stages of the session and also note the intended response.

Cool-Down

This component of the session comes at the end and allows time for participants to carry out exercises to assist the body in returning to its normal resting level in terms of heart rate, blood pressure, adrenalin levels and temperature. The cool-down will rid the body of waste material (lactic acid) as the legs will have a build-up of this waste following a training session or game. Participants should gradually reduce the intensity of the exercise in this phase and move from an upright to a position of rest on the floor with legs elevated to remove waste products. The cool-down should encompass 5–10 minutes of aerobic exercise and stretching exercises (which work on improving flexibility); a player must also refuel and rehydrate in this phase.

Differentiation

Differentiation can be defined as a process whereby the needs of individuals within a coaching session are recognized, planning by the coach takes place to meet those needs and appropriate activities are delivered in order to maximize learning and attainment for all individuals. Differentiation can be distinguished in terms of differentiation by task, for example where a coach plans a range of tasks which are of varying difficulty levels, and by outcome, for example when a range of challenges are set within the same activity and individuals respond according to their performance capabilities and level.

Differentiated strategies can relate to the content (the actual skills or strategies being delivered), to organization (the context of the session) and to the presentation of a coaching session (how the material is presented to a group or individual).

DIFFERENTIATION STRATEGIES

Organization	Grouping, space, roles and interaction
Presentation	Coaching style, response, resources and support
Content	Task, pace, level and practice style

Grouping

The size of a group can impact upon the effectiveness of the interactions and communication between members. A novice performer would benefit from smaller group activities where the communication channels and intellectual challenges are reduced. Smaller groups present a less pressurized situation for the novice and will enable the individual to engage in a learning activity with limited social comparison between group members.

Space

A coach can reduce or extend the working area for individuals in a session. For example, if a coach is working on an attacking task in a 2v2 situation, the space can be reduced to increase difficulty for the offensive players. With a reduced working area the offensive pair must get free from their opponent under greater pressure. If a coach witnesses a group struggling to succeed in getting free from their defence in this 2v2 practice, the space can be increased. Restricting a performer to a set area or zone can aid decision-making and often ensures all players have a greater involvement.

Roles

Within a game situation there is the opportunity for an individual within a coaching session to take on varying roles; positional roles, for example, can vary in complexity within a

Leadership roles in a group activity will challenge the more able participant.

game. In netball the more capable performer may take the lead role in calling a change in a defensive formation or strategy. Alternatively more able individuals may engage in the officiating or coach role within a session to promote greater understanding of the game.

Interaction

Novices will be more successful if they are allowed to practise a new skill in a cooperative environment. In a competitive situation, for example shooting under pressure, the novice is placed under immense pressure; this should initially be avoided.

Coaching Style

As previously noted, the more direct 'tell and show' style is more suitable for the novice. As performers move into the next stages of skill learning they can be exposed to a more empowering and questioning approach. The empowering style will allow the more able performer to engage in greater decision-making and identify a range of possible solutions to a task.

Response

Individuals within a coaching session can show their understanding and learning through demonstration, writing or through explanation. The more able performer may be comfortable in demonstrating a skill or solutions to a task to a group, whereas the less competent and confident performer may prefer to perform as part of a group. Individuals may also find it easier to explain their ideas rather than to perform them in a practice situation.

Resources

Equipment can be modified or adapted to increase success and provide the appropriate challenge. In netball a novice may practise with a size 4 (smaller ball) rather than the standard size 5 ball. Many games have a junior version of the game and this often means a smaller working area and/or modified rules.

Support

A novice performer or an individual who has a low attention span in a session would benefit from increased support from a coach or assistant. The effective coach should deploy any assistants to work with the groups requiring this extra attention.

Pace

Individuals working on learning activities in a coaching session may take varying amounts of time to complete them and often a coach working with a large group of performers will use work cards to support this strategy. If a coach groups by ability, then the number of challenges or tasks presented to each group can be increased or decreased given the performance level. The less able performers in a group should be given more time or a reduced number of options on a task in order to practise and achieve the outcome.

Level

A coach can set varying levels of challenge by devising a range of team sizes in a game situation. For example, less able performers will be more successful in a 3v3 game rather than a 5v5.

Practice Style

A novice performer will need to engage in practices that are less complex and involve the repetition of the same skill in a closed situation. A more able performer can cope with practising combinations of skills in a practice and is also able to cope in a range of more open contexts.

Differentiated activities represent one of the approaches outlined in an 'Inclusion

Spectrum' (Black and Haskins, 1996) and four other approaches have been highlighted to address the varying needs of a group. Although initially devised for Physical Education, the spectrum should be understood and applied by the coach and the approaches are outlined below:

- Mainstream activities: Total inclusion of all in a session
- Differentiated activities: Modified tasks
- Parallel activities: Same activity but ability grouping
- Adapted activities: All play adapted game
- Separate activities: All perform separately

A coach may implement one or a range of approaches in any one session in order to ensure inclusive coaching takes place. Varying the strategies to meet the needs of individuals in a group is recommended to promote greater challenge, learning and motivation. The effective coach will therefore coach the individuals within a session and not merely coach the sport.

To conclude, it is essential that the coach always puts the player first and this means placing the needs of participants before all other issues, such as a competition, parents and the coach's own individual goals and ambitions. The coach should ensure that all participants, whatever their age, ability or disability, are treated as individuals with their

Modifying the equipment and ball will help the young participant.

own specific needs, interests and goals. The coach must empower individuals and as a result ensure that they become responsible for their own learning and development.

53

CHAPTER 4

APPLICATION OF A GAME SENSE APPROACH
Alison Croad and Jose Castro

Game Sense is an approach that stresses the importance of promoting athletes' active engagement in their learning and decision-making. Indeed, the focus of Game Sense is to place the learner in situations in which decision-making and problem-solving en-

Focusing on technique in a game context is a beneficial method for coaches to adopt. Participants should be encouraged to problem-solve in game-based activities.

hance the player's learning and consequent performance. This is particularly relevant in a sport like netball due to its dynamic and complex nature as a team sport, with many changing variables and little time during quarter times to instruct guidance; a player with the ability to understand the game and be able to make appropriate decisions during the game, therefore, is vital.

This chapter explores the concept of Game Sense by first identifying the traditional approach to coaching and then discussing the benefits associated with a Game Sense approach and highlighting how it can be applied in a netball coaching context.

Traditional Approach to Coaching

The traditional approach to coaching places a large emphasis on technical skills, prioritizing them over tactical or cognitive skills. This is done by focusing on the technical skills in isolation from the game context and by assuming that mastering the technique is the first and main variable that a player needs to possess to be able to play the game successfully (see Fig. 4.1).

This method allows players to develop an understanding of the skill, but not how it can be applied in a game context. By introducing the technical skills step by step, players usually understand how the skill needs to be performed from a technical standpoint but lack an understanding of why they are doing it and how it would be applied in a game situation. This approach can therefore develop highly skilled performers who possess a range of specific techniques. However, their understanding of the game and their ability to make appropriate decisions in the game context are seriously compromised. This may lead to a wrong sense of success, as good coaching is more than developing good technical executors: it is about developing good players.

During this traditional approach the learner will assume a passive role, while the coach takes on an active and direct role, maintaining the control of the pace, sequence and content of the session. Moreover, by being passive recipients of the knowledge transmitted by the coach, the players are not being challenged to think, reflect and be critical. We are thus undermining the impact that coaching can have in developing the player as a whole. The traditional technique-based approach prevents coaches from developing a more all-rounded player, as it appears to neglect the cognitive process and problem-

More traditional practice styles isolate the skills from the game.

solving aspects required for successful game performance.

Game Sense

Game Sense is a game-based approach that challenges the notion that learning to play sport involves only refinement of skills isolated from the game context. It focuses on the game and not on the technique by using tactical aware-

```
┌─────────────────────────────────────────────┐
│      Skill Development (Technique focus)      │
└─────────────────────────────────────────────┘
                      ↓
┌─────────────────────────────────────────────┐
│      Skill Progression (Technique focus)      │
└─────────────────────────────────────────────┘
                      ↓
┌─────────────────────────────────────────────┐
│        Game Play (usually full game)          │
└─────────────────────────────────────────────┘
```

Fig. 4.1   The traditional approach to coaching.

TRADITIONAL APPROACH

You may coach a group the skill of a reverse pivot by isolating the skill using a feeder (F) and a worker (W) behind a cone or static defender a few metres away. The worker performs the skill of a reverse pivot and then runs out to receive a ball from the feeder.

   This skill can even be progressed to using a more active defender, encouraging a more dynamic pivot to get free. From this experience, will the performer be able to understand how or when to use this skill in a game environment? If taught through the traditional approach the skill is isolated from the game, and if this skill is progressed into a game environment you are likely to see either no attempt at all at using this skill or you will see it used continuously when not required due to a lack of understanding of why the skill may be useful within a game context.

---

ness to improve performance through the use of modified games. Learning is contextualized to game-like situations in which players are challenged to constantly interpret and adapt to a dynamic physical environment. Game Sense can make a contribution to the development of tactical understanding, decision-making and the ability to read the game. This approach also encourages players to understand why and what they are doing along with how to apply a skill in a game context. This is essentially achieved through the manipulation of the modified game forms applied in the session and through the coaching styles undertaken by the coach.

Therefore, Game Sense focuses on the use of modified games to develop game understanding and tactical awareness through setting up challenges and supporting players to problem-solve. The players are then questioned in order to allow them to reflect on their experience and formulate answers to the problems posed throughout the modified game. The answers to the problem are then developed further through skill development, which can be achieved through further game experiences. Game Sense as an approach is not normally depicted due to its evolving and fluid nature, but for the purpose of a direct comparison against the traditional approach, see Table 4.1.

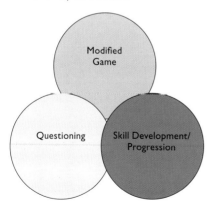

Fig. 4.2   The Game Sense approach.

Modified Games

Game Sense is a player-centred approach in which the players are empowered to have an active role in the process. However, this does not mean that the coach's role should be neglected. Instead, rather than act as a transmitter of objective knowledge, the coach should act as a facilitator, collaborating actively with the players in order to guide them in the learning process. Also, the coach should be the one creating appropriate opportunities

Table 4.1   Comparison between the traditional approach and the Game Sense approach.

Traditional technique-based approach	Game Sense approach
Skills are taught in isolation of the game	Skills are directly linked to the game – an understanding is developed of how and when to use them effectively
Players need to master the technical skills before they are able to play	Players start by playing the game and develop specific skills from their understanding of how they fit within the game
Activities can appear to the learner to be unrelated to each other	Skills are practised as a result of what arose during the modified game play
Coach-led	Player-centred approach
Low level of enjoyment	High level of enjoyment

for learning by manipulating the environment – for example, by modifying numbers, playing smaller games of 4v4, 3v3, 5v5 or an overload game with either extra defenders or extra attackers depending on what the focus is, such as 3v4. All of these games can be played in a smaller area, for example one third of the netball court. The coach can also modify the rules by restricting who can be passed to – for example, you cannot pass back to the player who has passed to you – or the type of pass being used, to encourage certain movements. Finally the coach can also make modifications in the equipment, by using different balls such as tennis balls, Frisbees, or even using more balls in a game. The learning environment should be adapted to the players' needs and level of tactical complexity in order to help each one's potential flourish.

In this sense, the coach should encourage players to participate in problem-solving situations and encourage them to 'engage in self-discovery'. Basically, by manipulating the constraints within the session, the coach will be stimulating the players to become critical thinkers and more autonomous, as, after all,

the players are the ones who have to make the decisions in the game, not the coach. They are the ones who need to have the ability to adapt to the game constraints in play. Also, if players are encouraged to think critically, to identify problems, to find solutions for those problems and share their thoughts about it, it will have positive outcomes on their motivation and ownership.

Game Sense is a variation of the Teaching Games for Understanding (TGfU) (Bunker and Thorpe, 1982) principle developed for the use of teaching physical education, with an emphasis on a more flexible and 'looser' approach. Despite the differences, the pedagogical principles applied in modified games for TGfU can also be applied in Game Sense. These principles include:

- **Modification of the game by representation**, which entails small-sided games that represent the formal game format, such as 4v4 and 5v5 games, played with basic netball rules such as no footwork, contact or obstruction, but with all players allowed to move around the

The coach should stand back and facilitate learning.

whole of the area. This allows the players to develop game understanding and self-reflection through their experience, which can be transferred easily from the small-sided game and relate directly to the full game.

- **Modification of the game by exaggeration**, which considers rules manipulation to exaggerate tactical problems. This can include modifications such as restricting overhead balls to encourage greater movement; this will allow players to experiment with different ways to get free to work out what works best for them and when. The idea of being able to lose your player is an important aspect in netball – a sport where you have a dedicated member of the opposite team playing against you.
- **Adjustment of tactical complexity**, which emphasizes the need to adapt tactical problems to the level of understanding and motor skills that the players possess. This can include a development

of basic passing or moving with modifications – for example, no passing back to the player who passed to you – or developing complex tactical approaches, such as the use of width by including wide channels in the game that have to be used before a team can score.

Questioning

A key strategy when coaching using the Game Sense approach is the use of questioning, which empowers the players and stimulates them to think and reflect on their experience. Game situations in training can be stopped at key moments identified by the coach in order to challenge the players to reflect on their performance. This process will engage the performer, prompt greater decision-making, and encourage the use of self-reflection and awareness while reviewing individual or team performance. The use of questioning will develop player-centred coaching that chal-

MODIFIED GAME EXAMPLES

Possession ball: 5v5 in a third of the netball court with normal netball playing rules, i.e. no footwork, contact or obstruction allowed. Six successful passes result in a goal and change of team in possession. The opposition can intercept, or an error (i.e. ball out of court or footwork), can result in turnover of play. The modification includes no overhead balls. This should result in the need for the attacking team to move to lose their defender and receive the ball. Change of direction and change of speed will be emphasized.

Hoop ball: Netball is played across the width of a third of a netball court in smaller teams, i.e. 4v4 or 5v5. There is a hoop or marked-out area in each corner of the area. Normal netball rules apply regarding footwork, contact and obstruction. Players pass amongst their team and they must score by catching in the hoop or marked-out area of two different hoops to register a point. This encourages a team to draw defenders away from certain areas to decide which hoop/area to attack and score in. Restrictions can also be added to enhance the tactical complexity by asking for a certain number of passes each time before the ball can be caught in a hoop or identified zone/area.

lenges the coach to move away from the centre of the learning process.

The questions posed should be designed to prompt analysis and greater application to the task at hand, and placing them in appropriate contexts will allow them to develop player autonomy. Open-ended questions are most effective at promoting decision-making, i.e. questions that do not involve a simple 'yes' or 'no' answer. Questions starting with 'what?' or 'tell me about' are more effective at prompting reflection on a situation or an event, encouraging further application of the player's knowledge and understanding.

Common issues that can occur during questioning include: lack of clarity, which prevents players developing the reflective connection to the experience they have just had; relying on the same respondent repeatedly, which prevents other individuals from feeling included in the reflective process; not allowing sufficient time to think and respond; and not providing a supportive environment to allow all players to feel they can offer an answer, even if it may not be correct. The coach should therefore consider these issues when questioning the group.

Skill Development Progression

The traditional technique-based approach consists of sessions with unrelated introductory activities, followed by the development and progression of an isolated technical skill whose purpose is unclear to the learners. Usually, these sessions end with a game form that is inappropriate to the ability of the majority. Consequently, this leads to a low percentage of participants succeeding when playing the game, while supposedly skilful players present inflexible techniques and poor decision-making capacity.

In contrast, Game Sense promotes appreciation and tactical awareness before developing technical skills, suggesting that the technical and tactical components of the game can be taught simultaneously. Moreover, the sessions should include activities built

Open-ended questioning by the coach will support the game-based approach.

on the knowledge developed in the previous game, in a logical progression from simple to more complex games.

Indeed, in the Game Sense approach learning is always located within games, and there is no prior identification of the skills to be developed. Technical work, far from being planned, is only done when the coach or teacher deems it necessary. It is, however, important to notice that simply applying small-sided games and mini-games does not mean that game-based approaches, such as

Game Sense, are being applied, as 'in themselves, mini-games are not progressive: we build up to them, pass through them and go beyond them' (Bunker & Thorpe, 1986, p.58). The design is important, but the main aspect is the focus, i.e. the principles of play, and the players' decision-making based on tactical awareness. The tactical problems should evolve in their complexity, according to the players' tactical understanding. In the context of game-based approaches, such as Game Sense, performance is usually related to the level of the game form played. In this sense, the players' learning is judged in terms of the technical and tactical complexity.

In netball it is important that a young player is introduced to the game principles in attack and defence. A player should not only develop the technical skills for the game, but also learn how to execute these by applying the following principles of play.

Attacking Principles

- **Score goals:** The ultimate aim of a game is to score a goal and in netball there are only two playing positions that can do this (Goal Shooter and Goal Attack). The two shooters in the game must be able to shoot under pressure and when they are being defended. Games need to be modified to allow players time to practise in training, executing a movement to receive

---

TIPS FOR QUESTIONING

- Use questions that require a response greater than a simple yes or no.
- Questions that start with 'What…?' or 'Tell me about…' will prompt reflection. For example, 'What was your team doing well in defence to prevent the opposition from scoring?' Or, 'Tell me about what your team was doing in that game to be successful.'
- Good questioning should: focus attention, invite enquiry, assess knowledge and understanding, develop self- and peer-assessment skills and relate to the practice or session focus.

the ball in a prime shooting position which is nearer to the post.

- **Provide options for the ball carrier:** There should always be three passing options available to the ball carrier and it is often preferable to have two forward options and a lateral option. The ball carrier must make the correct decision about who to pass to based upon the position of the defenders, the space available and the timing of the mover to receive (if too early or too late this could affect the successful receipt of the pass). Games can be modified to develop options, for example with fewer defenders so there is always a free player to encourage the player to make the correct decision.

- **Be ball side:** The receiver should remain between the ball carrier and the opponent as it is harder for a defender to intercept in this situation. The ball carrier can pass the ball faster and more directly into the hands of the receiver in this instance. If games are developed that prevent any overhead balls, this can encourage players to move to be ball side.

- **Pass on the straight line:** This is the most direct route from the ball carrier to the receiver and is also the fastest route to goal. By passing on the straight line there is less of an angle for defenders to intercept. A long diagonal ball allows more time for a defender to move into the line of the pass for the interception. Games can work on grids or channels to develop this and ensure players pass to a straight line option.

COURT BALANCE

The following will aid a player's understanding of court balance and can be developed at different levels in modified games.

- If there are two players moving in the same space to take a pass, the court could not have been balanced. More tactically aware players should be able to read off players in front of them to prevent this.
- The ball should travel in straight lines (not diagonals across the court).
- A player must often lead a defender out of the main space to receive the ball or allow a team-mate to receive the ball.
- A ball carrier must turn to face the direction of play to sight passing options early.
- The pass should be delivered in the space ahead of the receiver.
- The receiver must time her movement in order to receive on the straight line.
- Players may decide to interchange roles – for example, the Goal Attack may drop into the shooting circle and the Goal Shooter may move out and become involved in the play within the attacking third to create different options on court.

Coaching Points to Develop Spatial Awareness
- Scan the area for important cues
- Player at the front initiates
- Alert to all players' intentions
- Clear space for team-mates and maintain court balance
- Execution of the pass and a well-timed movement

- **Use a square (lateral) pass to a player on the overlap run:** If the forward options are not available to the ball carrier, there should be an option to pass the ball square to a player moving from behind. This ensures that the attacking players in front of the ball carrier are not drawn up the court so as to cause problems with the subsequent passes to goal. This square pass can also open up the court and width available to the attacking team and can be developed by applying restrictions in a modified game of 'one pass forward, one pass sidewards' and restricting where players can move – for example, the side pass has to go to someone moving from behind the ball carrier.

- **Penetrate space:** All players in the game must recognize the space principles in order to create space for themselves and others. Defenders will try to restrict the space available and therefore make attempts to disrupt play. All players must be able to scan the area for important cues, and as the ball is caught the ball carrier should observe the position of the defenders in relation to her team-mates. This principle can be covered in many ways depending on the tactical complexity of the players. To achieve an effective attacking play and use the space available there is a need to balance the court. If the attacking players can balance the court, they will be providing more than one option for the ball carrier by creating space for themselves and for others in their team to use.

Defending Principles

- **Gain possession:** A team can only score goals by regaining possession and the defending team must ensure that it makes every attempt to gain an interception, to force the opposition into error or to rebound a missed shot. This can be developed in game play by overloading defenders or restricting the areas attackers can receive passes.

- **Be ball side:** The defender must strive to gain the ball side position, which means being between the ball carrier and the opponent. In this position the ball carrier is often forced to send a higher trajectory pass, allowing more time for a defender to move into the path of the ball and intercept. As with the attacking principle, if a game is played preventing overhead balls, the defender will realize the best option is to try and stay ball side of the attacker to prevent the attacker from receiving.

- **Apply pressure:** The defending players must apply sufficient pressure on the attacking players to force an error and ultimately to regain possession. The defenders will be striving to gain an interception otherwise known as a turnover. The three stages of defence must be applied successfully by the team so as to ensure pressure is placed upon the ball carrier and potential receivers of the next pass. Applying pressure can be done through:

- **Reducing the options available to the ball carrier:** The attacking team will try to provide choices for the ball carrier and it is the defence who must try and counteract this. By reducing the options available, there is a chance that the ball carrier will make a passing error or hold the ball for more than 3 seconds. The defending players should communicate with each other to ensure all passing options are closed down and the space for the attacking players to move into is also limited. The defender should close off any options on the straight line and try to force a longer diagonal pass that is more challenging for the ball carrier to execute and often more easily intercepted.

- **Restricting the space available to the attacking players:** The defender should work hard to force the attacking player into a difficult area to receive the pass – for example, close to a side or back line or near a third line which is the boundary for an area the attacker is not able to move into. Closing down space can be achieved by the defence marking the receivers on ball side and also by a defender marking the ball carrier. Modified games can reward defenders who apply pressure and force play into certain areas to again encourage this action and for players to 'try out' what the best way to do this is. The defending players in a small-sided game can be awarded a point if they force the carrier to hold the ball for 3 seconds, if they intercept, or if they force the players into areas marked out on court as this will encourage tighter defending.

A defender applying pressure to try and force the error.

Summary

In conclusion, Game Sense is a challenging approach, but also an extremely meaningful and rich one. It is challenging in the sense that it demands a greater knowledge of the sport and its pedagogical endeavours, so that all the content can be coached in an empowering way around game-based situations. Nevertheless, by doing this, the players will be encouraged to develop their technical, tactical and cognitive skills in a more meaningful and realistic learning context. Furthermore, this will promote tactical awareness, decision-making and enjoyment.

As the players gain ownership and a 'voice' in the process, the coach's role can become more that of a facilitator. The coach, though, is still the person orchestrating the process, and needs to possess a level of knowledge and skill that is sufficient to develop and strengthen players' all-round performance.

CHAPTER 5

COACHING THE TECHNICAL SKILLS IN NETBALL
Anita Navin

Movement Skills

Fundamental movement skills provide the backbone for the effective execution of specific skills in netball and indeed a player's success in the sport. The movement skills should be developed in the early stages of an individual's training and developed during the primary school years. A coach must continue to integrate movement skills into any coaching session for all ages. Progressive practices should initially isolate the movement aspect of any netball skill, allowing individuals an opportunity to work on their movement repertoire without the pressure of the ball being present.

Take-Off

The take-off is the first step required to initiate a movement either from a moving or stationary position. An individual will make a conscious decision to move and it is the ability of the individual to execute this first step effectively that will maximize the speed of the response. Working on this initial take-off step maximizes the chance of beating an opponent to the ball.

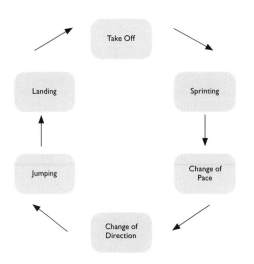

COACHING POINTS

- Feet shoulder-width apart.
- Opposite arm to leg drives forward.
- Body upright and balanced with weight over feet.
- Head up, looking ahead.
- High knee lift to initiate the take-off step.

Fig. 5.1   The netball movement skills.

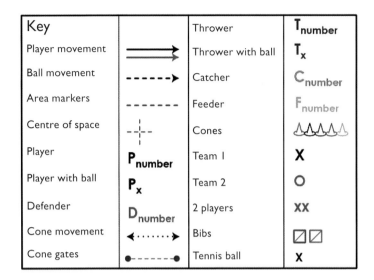

Key		Thrower	T_{number}
Player movement	→	Thrower with ball	T_x
Ball movement	- - - - ->	Catcher	C_{number}
Area markers	- - - - - - -	Feeder	F_{number}
Centre of space	--+--	Cones	ΛΛΛΛ
Player	P_{number}	Team 1	X
Player with ball	P_x	Team 2	O
Defender	D_{number}	2 players	XX
Cone movement	◄ ······ ►	Bibs	☐☐
Cone gates	●- - - - -●	Tennis ball	X

This key covers all the practices in this section.

COMMON ERRORS
- Knee lift not high enough.
- Hips not leaning for-wards in the direction of the movement.
- Stepping back before going forward.

COACHING POINTS

- Keep weight on balls of feet.
- Head up and upper body upright.
- Opposite arm to leg, with arms bent at 90 degrees.
- Feet shoulder-width apart.
- High knee lift.

Sprinting
The ability to move at speed is an essential skill in netball and the ability to change pace and direction must also be trained. Players should combine an effective take-off with a sprint to ensure they move as quickly as possible through the court when on attack and defence.

COMMON ERRORS
- Arms are not synchro-nized with the leg action.
- Stride length is too long and more than a shoul-der-width distance.
- The knee lift is too low.

Change of Direction
A change of direction is effective when trying to deceive an opponent and when the attacker moves in one direction but then stops and cuts back in another.

COACHING POINTS

- Feet shoulder-width apart.
- Weight over the feet.
- Upper body is balanced over the feet and upright.
- Initiate the change of direction with a strong plant of the outside foot.
- Strong push-off from the outside foot speeds up the directional change and the inside foot leads.
- Hips and shoulders turn quickly to accelerate in the new direction.

COMMON ERRORS

- Upper body dips downwards when the foot is planted to change direction.
- A long stride is used leading into the foot plant to change direction.
- Hips are slow to turn into the direction of the movement.

A practice to support the development of the sprinting technique:

The players will work on their capacity to process information and move at speed to receive the ball.

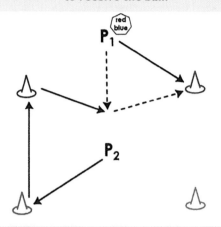

PRACTICE OUTCOMES

- To use a sprint and change of direction.

- To pass ahead of the receiver within the space.

- To pass the ball flat and fast.

- To focus on the ball at all times.

- To move on to the ball at speed.

- To use a range of passing options.

TASK/GROUP ORGANIZATION

Four coloured cones are required and players work in half of a third area.

PI calls two colours and P2 must move to both cones before receiving a pass from PI in the centre of the space.

PI must then move to receive a pass at one of the coloured cones not used by P2 (in this example she moves to green).

The practice restarts with PI at green.

PROGRESSIONS AND DIFFERENTIATION

PI and P2 can pass the ball four times, moving to a coloured cone with all cones having been covered after the four passes.

The practice is easier when calling one colour only.

POTENTIAL QUESTION TO POSE

What must the mover focus upon in the practice and how can she do this?

(Answer: The ball and by angling the upper body when moving away.)

Change of Pace

A change of pace is often executed to displace a defender, allowing the player to receive the ball in an uncontested space. Elite performers will effectively use a moderate pace as the opponent tracks them through a space and then suddenly accelerate to get free. A change of pace can also be accompanied by a change of direction to effectively outwit an opponent.

COACHING POINTS

- Keep body upright with good body balance and alignment.
- Use small steps to allow for a sudden change of pace.
- Pump the arms to accelerate.
- Keep weight over feet when decreasing the pace.

COMMON ERRORS

- Stride length too big when increasing the pace.
- Limited use of the arms when accelerating.
- Body not balanced over the feet.
- Upper body dips when accelerating.

Changing direction involves a push off the outside foot.

Jumping

Often players will jump from stationary and moving positions, which does necessitate jumping off one or two feet. Coaches should ensure that young performers experience and practise the five basic jumps, which are:

- jumping from two feet to land on two feet
- jumping from one foot to land on the same foot
- jumping from two feet to land on one foot
- jumping from one foot to land on the other foot
- jumping from one foot to land on two feet

Netball is an aerial game with several passes being caught in the air, and jumping is a vital movement skill for a player receiving a pass or when defending a high ball. There is also a need for players to jump and extend forwards to take a ball at speed.

COACHING POINTS FOR JUMPING UPWARDS

- Use a two-footed base where possible.
- Feet shoulder-width apart.
- Lower the hips but keep the body upright.
- Arms swing back and vigorously upwards.
- Maintain a straight body position in the air.

COACHING POINTS FOR JUMPING FORWARDS

- Bend knees, lower hips but keep body upright.
- Swing arms, lowering and driving the body forward.
- Keep head up.

A practice to support the development of the change of direction and change of pace:

Four players move within an area that has five spaces defined.

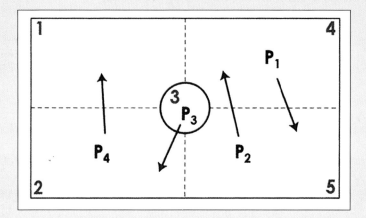

PRACTICE OUTCOMES

- To use their vision to move into a free space.

- To change of pace and direction.

- To use peripheral vision and read off the front player to locate the next available space.

- To see the whole space.

TASK/GROUP ORGANIZATION

Use a third of the court.

Define the area into five spaces, or ensure there is always one more space in relation to the number of players in the area.

Players can only spend up to 3 seconds in a space.

Work for 30 seconds.

PROGRESSIONS AND DIFFERENTIATION

Defence can be added to two areas to track the attackers and attempt to delay them for more than 3 seconds.

Players must execute a different method of getting free in each space prior to moving on.

POTENTIAL QUESTION TO POSE

When moving in this practice what should the player have in their vision?

(Answer: Should be able to see all players and the whole space.)

The ability to jump upwards and extend forward to catch the ball is important.

COMMON ERRORS

- Limited arm movement in the direction of the jump.
- Hips do not lower sufficiently for the upwards jump.
- Knees are not flexed on take-off.

Landing

The ability to land is an essential skill to accompany a jump, particularly when considering the footwork rule that applies in netball. Landing effectively is crucial in terms of preventing injury and a coach will always spend a great deal of time on developing this technique.

COMMON ERRORS

- Landing on the heels or flat-footed.
- Not flexing the knees.
- Body leaning forward over the feet.

COACHING POINTS

- Flex knees and slightly flex ankles on impact.
- Land on the balls of the feet.
- Keep upper body upright, abdominals tight and head upright.
- If landing on one foot bring the other down as quickly as possible to ensure balance and control.

Side Step

The use of a side step is an essential movement skill that will enhance a player's ability to get free, move around and also track an opponent when defending. The use of a side step will allow circle players to move in various directions in an attempt to outwit an opponent within a confined space. Defending through all areas of the court involves tracking a player from in front, and often the lateral movement means a side step may be used.

COACHING POINTS

- Keep on the balls of the feet.
- Head up.
- Knees slightly flexed with the trunk upright.
- Feet should remain shoulder-width apart.
- Weight should be balanced over the feet.

COMMON ERRORS
- Feet beyond shoulder-width.
- Weight falls over the outside foot.

Turning in the Air

Jumping and landing are the essential skills that support the ability to turn in the air. Players will use a turn in the air to ensure that on landing they face the direction of play and the attacking goal. The ball carrier in netball has only 3 seconds to make a deci-sion and pass or shoot. If a player can jump and turn in the air before landing, this will allow more time to observe the options available and make the appropriate deci-sion. Turning in the air removes the need to pivot after landing to face the direction of play.

COACHING POINTS

- Use the coaching points for jumping.
- After take-off begin to initiate the turn with the head, shoulders and hips turn-ing.
- Keep body upright; abdominals should be tight.
- Maintain the balanced body position on landing.

COMMON ERRORS
- Not turning the hips after take-off, and initiating the turn early.

The movement skills outlined in this section will support the development of all the specific skills required in netball. The ability to move

Players will use the side step to track or get free from an opponent.

efficiently requires effective technique accompanied by the required level of fitness. All of the movement skills outlined require good physical conditioning and players must work hard to ensure they are fast, strong and powerful.

Individual Netball Skills

Netball is physiologically demanding and players must exercise a high level of skill, employing passing, catching and shooting skills in an ever-changing tactical and pressurized environment. An individual must also be able to make accurate decisions in terms of when, where and why a particular skill is executed. For example, what type of pass will be best to use in this situation? How will you decide when to release the ball? Or what are your passing options?

This section will present an overview of the following skills:

- Catching (two-handed and one-handed)
- Chest pass
- Bounce pass
- Shoulder pass
- Overhead pass
- Shooting

Catching

For the static two-handed catch, players must prepare to catch by keeping their eyes on the ball, moving their body to meet the ball and extending their arms towards the ball.

At the execution phase of the catch, players must have their fingers spread around the back and sides of the ball and must squeeze onto the ball. The thumbs are in the middle; with the first fingers ensure there is a 'W' shape behind the ball. The hands and arms 'give' on contact and the ball is brought into the body in preparation to throw.

KEY COACHING POINTS

- Eyes on the ball.
- Fingers spread.
- 'W' shape with thumbs and first finger behind the ball.
- 'Give' on contact with the arms and hands.

When catching a ball two-handed on the move, players must keep their heads up and jump to catch in order to control the momentum. They must land in a balanced position with their weight over the landing foot or both feet. The hips should be lowered and the knees flexed to provide more stability and control to the landing position.

Often a player will catch the ball and turn simultaneously in the air in order to face the direction of play. This means the player does not need to pivot after landing and therefore has more time to process information and make a decision over who to pass to. For this to be executed correctly a player must drive up and extend towards the ball with feet off the ground, ensuring that the turn begins at the take-off point. To initiate the turn the player must take off by pushing in the direction of the turn and should move head, shoulders and hips in the intended direction.

On occasions within the game there is a need to catch one-handed, particularly if the ball is out to the side of the body and at a greater distance away from the body. Players will extend their catching arm and hand towards the ball and as soon as possible they will add the second hand as the ball is brought into the body. A player must also 'give' when catching to absorb the impact. The ball is controlled by the fingers spread around the ball. A coach should ensure that players

A practice to develop the catching technique:

**Players have a tennis ball and must retrieve the ball after only one bounce,
working their hand-eye coordination for catching.**

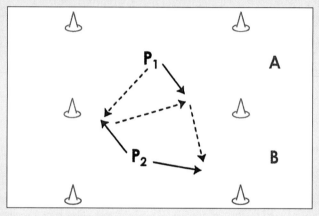

PRACTICE OUTCOMES

- To move at speed to collect the tennis ball after no more than one bounce.

- To try to outwit the opponent using a fake or the eyes to deceive.

- To locate and pass effectively to the free space in the opponent's half of the area.

TASK/GROUP ORGANIZATION

Two zones are marked out using six cones.

Players use an underarm throw and the ball must be released in an upwards motion when aiming for a space in the opponent's half.

A point is scored if the opponent does not receive the ball after one bounce, or if the ball is thrown out of the area.

PROGRESSIONS AND DIFFERENTIATION

Use a smaller area to make it harder for the players to throw into a space.

Play a 2v2.

Use a netball and a range of passes.

POTENTIAL QUESTION TO POSE

Why is the speed of release important in this practice?

(Answer: The defender may be repositioning and has less time to react on a fast release.)

Catching on the move must be practised in the early years.

develop the ability to catch one-handed with both the right and left hand.

Throwing

All players must develop their throwing skills by developing competence in the full range of throws. A throw is only successful in the game if the ball carrier has made the correct decision and addresses the many perceptual factors.

PERCEPTUAL FACTORS

- What type of pass to use – is it a short or long distance pass?
- Who do I pass to given more than one option?
- Where do I pass?
- What weight of pass to use – is it a flat, fast pass or lofted in the air?
- When should the ball be thrown?

For the successful execution of all throws there are some common coaching points that should be stressed to any player. Players should always keep their eyes on the target, keep their body balanced throughout the pass and also follow through with the arms and hands towards the target.

The Chest Pass

The chest pass is most commonly used over shorter distances when a defender is not between the ball carrier and receiver. It allows the player to send a flat, fast pass that is easily controlled. The pass starts from the two-handed catching position with the ball being held at chest height. In the preparation phase the fingers must be spread behind the ball, keeping the elbows low and relaxed. In the execution phase the body weight is transferred forwards and the ball is released as the arms and wrists extend. Players must follow through with their hands, fingers and arms.

A practice to develop the passing techniques in netball:

Two players pass and move in the space, receiving the ball in all areas and testing passing accuracy by aiming for the colour called out.

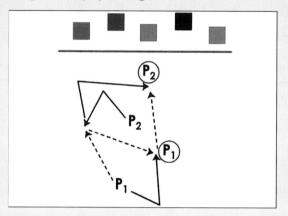

PRACTICE OUTCOMES

- To pass ahead of the moving player.

- To extend the arms to catch on the move.

- To execute an accurate pass.

TASK/GROUP ORGANIZATION

Five pieces of card are stuck on the wall.

PI and P2 move the ball in the space using a double lead.

The area of work should be defined using spot markers if necessary.

The coach or a static player in the group will call a colour and the player in possession must aim to hit the marker on the wall from their location.

Repeat four times, then rest.

PROGRESSIONS AND DIFFERENTIATION

The call is made when the player is furthest away from the wall (harder).

The player can use a give and go with the other player to get nearer the wall before aiming for the colour (easier).

POTENTIAL QUESTION TO POSE

What part of the body is important for accuracy in passing?

(Answer: Focus on the target, step to the target when passing and follow through in the direction of the target.)

- Ball is held at chest height.
- Elbows low and relaxed.
- Maintain 'W' shape used when catching.
- Transfer body weight forwards when throwing.
- Extend the arms and wrists on the follow-through.

The Bounce Pass

The two-handed bounce pass is used over short distances and is most commonly employed by players when passing to someone in a confined space – for example, a Wing Attack or Centre passing on the circle edge to a shooter inside the shooting circle. This type of pass works effectively against tall defence players who have strength in their ability to intercept and challenge any aerial ball being sent to a shooter. In the preparation phase the ball is held just below chest height and applies a similar action to the chest pass. In the execution phase the ball should bounce two thirds of the distance between the ball carrier and receiver with the bounce often being kept low to prevent a defender intercepting the pass.

On occasions a one-handed bounce pass is used, which does enable the player to obtain a better angle for the pass and also to protect the ball from a defender. In the preparation phase the ball is taken to the side of the body and kept at waist height. To execute the one-handed pass the player takes a step across with the opposite foot to the throwing arm.

The Shoulder Pass

This pass is used over longer distances and requires considerable power. In the preparation phase the ball carrier takes up a balanced starting position with the opposite foot forwards in relation to the throwing arm. The ball is positioned just above the shoulder with fingers spread behind the ball. A young or novice player may use the second hand to steady the ball prior to executing the pass. The ball is positioned behind the shoulder to ensure that maximum power is gained. As the ball is released the hips rotate as the hand, arm and shoulder move forwards towards the receiver. The body weight is transferred forwards in the direction of the pass and onto the front foot. In the follow-through the arm, hand and fingers extend towards the target.

- Ball held above and behind the shoulder.
- Opposite foot forwards to throwing arm.
- As the ball is released the hips rotate.
- On execution the hand, arm and shoulder extend forwards.

Overhead Pass

This pass allows the ball carrier to clear a defender's reach and can be high, floating or straight. The ball is held above the head and the position of the fingers and hands is the same as for the two-handed catch. The ball is taken slightly behind the head with the wrists extended backwards in the preparation phase. As the ball is released the arms extend to propel the ball forward to the receiver. The power for this throw is from the elbows as the arm extends.

A practice to develop shooting technique:

The shooter must move around the markers before receiving a pass and executing the shot.

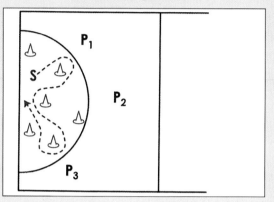

PRACTICE OUTCOMES

- To move efficiently around the markers, maintaining an upright body position.
- To move to a different-coloured marker each time.
- To use and change the body angle to sight the ball at all times.
- To use a strong take-off on the change of direction.
- To execute a shot at the end of the sprint to the post.

TASK/GROUP ORGANIZATION

Work in the goal circle and use six markers of varying colours.

PI–P3 pass the ball continuously.

PI–P3 can pass to the shooter at any point and when moving to the post.

The shooter should cover at least two markers before receiving the ball.

If the shooter gets the rebound another shot can be executed – repeat ×6.

Work for 30 seconds.

PROGRESSIONS AND DIFFERENTIATION

Defenders can shadow in the circle.

Another shooter can be added.

PI–3 complete four passes in the third before a pass to the shooter.

POTENTIAL QUESTION TO POSE

What makes a good body angle when moving between markers?

(Answer: Upper body should face the ball so as to be able to see most of the space at all times.)

Shooting

There are several shooting styles across the world and the preferred techniques have changed from a two-handed shot to the one-handed high release shot. Australian shooting legend Margaret Caldow devised the one-handed high release technique that now dominates the game. It must be noted that the Caribbean nations follow the technique implemented by Trinidadian shooter Jean Pierre, who played at international level and competed in five consecutive World Championships. In this Caribbean style the shooting arm starts much lower than the Australian style but is released at a similar point. The stance is different, with the Caribbean shot having the shooting foot placed forward with weight on the back foot in contrast to the stance being parallel with feet shoulder-width apart.

It is the Australian high release shot that is adopted and coached within the UK's development and international programmes. This style allows a shooter to clear the ball away from a defender. In the preparation phase the shooter should note the following technical points:

- Body balanced, with feet hip-width apart and back straight.
- Ball held high above the head with the ball resting on the fingers of the shooting hand.
- Wrist under the ball and fingers facing backwards.
- The second hand is used to steady the ball by positioning it on the side of the ball.
- Eyes focused on the front of the ring and ball to be lifted above this point.

At the execution phase:

- Wrist should drop slightly behind the head.
- Use the index finger to guide the shot with a little backspin.
- Use knees and ankles to push ball upwards and forwards to goal.
- The ball should lift high over the front of the ring and for a clean shot should begin to drop into the goal at the midpoint above the ring.

In the follow-through the index finger should point forwards and slightly downwards.

Encourage the second hand to be positioned at the side of the ball when shooting.

A practice to develop attacking skills:

Attacking players must use a different attacking move when approaching a marker and offload to a feeder when all have received a pass.

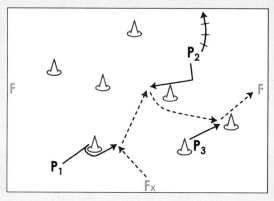

PRACTICE OUTCOMES

- To use a range of attacking moves when getting free.

- To move towards the ball carrier on the straight line to receive.

- To clear as a front player to create space for others.

- To communicate on attack and read the cues to indicate readiness to receive a pass.

TASK/GROUP ORGANIZATION

Use a half of the third area.

Six to eight markers are randomly placed.

Three static feeders around the outside of the practice space.

Three attacking players show different attacking moves at the markers, not repeating one in succession (30 seconds).

After all have received it, the ball goes to a feeder and the front player must clear (P2 above).

PROGRESSIONS AND DIFFERENTIATION

Feeders move around the outside.

After one rotation of six passes a feeder comes in to be a defender.

POTENTIAL QUESTION TO POSE

Where should the front player clear?

(Answer: Away from the other attackers and not in the line of the next intended pass.)

Shooters may implement their footwork skills and use the rules to their advantage by taking a step backwards, forwards or to the side when in the act of shooting. If a defender is placing a great deal of pressure on the shooter, the step backwards and to the side can counteract this pressure and give the shooter more space to release the ball. Such steps can also be used when throwing the ball to relieve pressure being forced on you by the defender and to gain an advantage.

The step forwards is used when the defender is not positioned in front of you, allowing you the chance to move closer to the post. This is most commonly seen in a penalty shot situation when your opponent is standing by your side until the ball is released.

Once the basic shooting technique has been mastered, a player can begin to use the step. When executing the step it is vital that the body weight is rebalanced over the foot you have stepped on. Balance must be maintained throughout the action and follow-through.

TIPS FOR SHOOTING

- Master the technique by practising daily.
- Body balance is crucial.
- Use the stepping techniques to gain an advantage.
- Remember your landing foot when using the step techniques.

Netball rules permit only two players to shoot in a match, these being the Goal Attack and Goal Shooter, hence it is vital that they have a high percentage success rate. Both must have confidence in their ability and must have the qualities to cope well under pressure.

Attacking Skills

Attacking players must be able to get free from a stationary and moving position within the game, using their vision and powers of decision-making to identify a suitable front or back space to move into. Experienced performers will be autonomous in their execution of the skills and will be able to demonstrate the ability to vary the attacking skills used according to the tactical and technical strengths and weaknesses of the opposition. In game conditions players must also be able to read the necessary cues around them, work to get free under pressure and ultimately execute a well-timed move into the available free space.

It is vital that a coach offers practices that work to enhance a player's decision-making powers; this can be achieved by adding the perceptual factors into the training programme.

THE PERCEPTUAL FACTORS

- Space: where do I move?
- Timing: when to move and at what point do I break free?
- Pace: what speed and should the pace change to break free?
- Direction: should I move straight or diagonally? Forwards or backwards?

The attacking skills often incorporate one or more of the following movement skills: sprinting, and changes of pace and direction. The sprint to receive the ball is commonly referred to as a 'lead'. Some of the most important methods used to get free are outlined below:

- straight and diagonal lead
- double lead
- dodge and double dodge
- protecting a space

The Straight and Diagonal Lead

The correct sprinting technique should be applied to this attacking move and the player must focus ahead on the ball and the available space. The initial take-off is important and the attacker must use a high knee lift to gain momentum to move away from the defender. The direction of the lead is dependent upon the position of the defender(s) and, if the defence are marking from a side position, the player will often execute a diagonal move. Often defence will mark from the in-front position and a player may then decide to lead to the back space (either diagonally or straight). Players must practise the diagonal lead from both sides and in a forward and backwards direction. It is also important to practise this lead by taking off on the inside and outside foot. The outside foot take off allows the attacker to drive out quickly on the diagonal and away from the defender. The inside foot take-off allows the attacker to cut off the movement path of the defender.

The Double Lead

A double lead is executed if on the first lead the ball has not been received. A double lead often combines the attacking sprint with a change of direction and can be used to commit a defender in one direction before moving into a free space. This lead requires a convincing body movement and is often effective when the defender is persistent and marking tightly one on one. If executed quickly it ultimately leaves the defender out of position and opens up a space to receive the pass in.

The various combinations open up the forward or back space for the attacker and the up and back lead combination is useful when the defender has maintained a strong defensive position as the attacker has moved up the court. This move can also open up space when there is a potentially crowded situation. The change of direction at the end

of the first lead must be implemented when the ball carrier is ready to release the ball. If moving backwards, the attacker must maintain vision on the ball in order to monitor the flight and to time the jump to receive.

The Feint Dodge

The dodge can be used to free an opponent and is often executed when the defender is marking very tightly one on one and often from an in-front position. The dodge demands that the attacker executes a feint movement in one direction – often stated as 'selling a dummy to the defender' – before moving in another direction. This method is often used by players to get free from a stationary position and demands a good balanced body position. The attacker feints a movement to one side by planting the foot and using an upper body movement by the leading shoulder before moving off in the other direction. The feint must be strong and convincing without the attacker shifting all of the body weight in the direction of this first move. A powerful turn of the hips will initiate a fast movement into another direction to find a free space.

Protecting a Space

There are instances in the game when an attacker may wish to protect a space to receive the ball rather than execute a lead or dodge. This is most commonly seen within the goal circle where a shooter works to hold the position by making slight adjustments with the feet to ensure the defender keeps away from the space. The attacker must maintain a strong body position with knees flexed and a base slightly wider than shoulder-width to maintain stability. Timing of the move to receive is critical in this skill and the ball carrier will have released the ball before the attacker makes the move. The attacker will hold the position up close to the defender until the last possible moment and will then either lunge, jump or reach to receive the ball, keeping a position between the ball and defender. The pass must be accurate and consideration should be given to the strengths of the defender in order to decide which pass is the most effective. A defender who has good elevation and intercepts well in the air would be restricted by a bounce pass being placed into the space.

While in possession, any team must work to provide at least two forward options and one square option. Attackers will apply the relevant method of getting free following the evaluation of their opponent's strengths and the space available. The attacking move executed can split the defenders and free up space for a fellow team-mate to receive the ball. This does mean there could be up to three players moving and attempting to get free and these players must have good vision to ensure that they offer for the ball in a different space. Communication and team work are therefore essential between players. The following SPACE principles will support players in using their attacking skills to best effect in a game.

TOP TIPS

Scan the area for important cues
Player at the front initiates
Alert to all players' intentions
Clearing space for team-mates and maintaining court balance
Execution of the pass and a well-timed movement

Defending Skills

Each of the seven players on the court is required to defend and each must be able to demonstrate the ability to defend both on the receiver and on the ball. When marking the receiver the defender must shadow the attacker and restrict and prevent her from moving into the desirable space. When defending on the ball a player can influence the accuracy, direction, pace and height of the pass. By placing pressure on the ball the defender should limit the options by restricting the ball carrier's vision to locate the mover and passing space. In netball there are three stages of defence whereby a player makes attempts to gain an interception (see below). When defending, a player should make a quick transition from one stage to the next, for example: one on one marking – pressure on the ball – restrict the player. At all times the player is trying to gain possession by forcing the receiver or ball carrier into an error.

STAGES OF DEFENCE

Stage 1 Marking a player without the ball
Stage 2 Marking a player in possession of the ball
Stage 3 Restricting the player movement

Stage One Defence

The aim of stage one defence is to mark a player closely to prevent the player from receiving the ball or to gain an interception. If the ball is moving down the court defenders must constantly move around their opponent and reposition as the ball switches from side to side. Defenders must try to ensure that their opponent is not an option for the ball carrier. When a player is moving to get free from a dead ball situation, e.g. centre pass or throw-in, the defender must shadow the attacker and position very close to this player. The defender in this stage will try to intercept, force an uncontrolled receipt of the ball or force an out of court.

KEY COACHING POINTS

- Feet shoulder-width apart.
- Weight balanced on balls of feet.
- Arms flexed at front or side of body.
- Head up.
- Watch player and ball with your back to the player.
- Position within an arm's reach of the attacker.
- Defender half covers the attacking player.
- Body slightly angled to player's uncovered side.

Stage Two Defence

If an opponent receives the ball the defender must then put pressure on the ball carrier and mark the pass from a distance of 0.9 metre from the attacker's landing foot. Defenders will at times drop back from 0.9 metre to cover the immediate space near the ball carrier. Therefore, the aim of stage two is to apply pressure and restrict the vision of the ball carrier. The defender will try to intercept the pass, to tip the ball or force a weak pass. There are two approaches within this stage and defenders must decide whether to: a) keep their feet on the ground and cover the ball and space with their outstretched arms and hands; or b) choose to cover the ball but prepare to jump when the ball is released from the thrower. A defender who has good elevation and a well-timed jump will use approach b) to try for an interception. Circle defence will often use a combination of both approaches to try and force the shooters into making an error, while players defending through the court will prefer to keep their feet grounded so that they can recover and deny space should they not gain possession. Defenders must read the cues from the passer and assess the best approach to implement by asking themselves the following questions:

- Is my opponent taller than me?
- Does my opponent release the ball from a low position?
- If I am unsuccessful in stage two can my player gain ground away from me and be a key option for her team?
- Does the shooter miss when I lean or when I jump?
- If I defend further back from 0.9 metre does this force a slower pass for my team-mates to intercept?

The defender should influence the direction and height of the pass if an interception cannot be gained and this may allow a defender marking the receiver to intercept. Following an assessment of their opponent, defenders should select the best arm position to cover the ball, the distance they should stand from their opponent, and their shoulder/body alignment in relation to the ball carrier and receiver.

KEY COACHING POINTS FOR STAGE TWO

- Take up position 0.9 metre in front of player as quickly as possible.
- One arm extended over the ball and one covering the main space.
- On the balls of the feet.
- Feet shoulder-width apart.
- Knees flexed if executing a jump to defend.
- Head up, watching the ball and ball carrier's eyes.
- If jumping anticipate the release point.
- Jump up and towards the player for the interception.

Stage Three Defence

This stage is also known as restrictive marking and the aim is to prevent opponents from moving to their desired space on the court. A successful stage three defender will ensure

A practice for developing the stages of defence:

Players work in pairs and together to deny space, track attacking players to limit their options and create opportunities to gain possession or force errors.

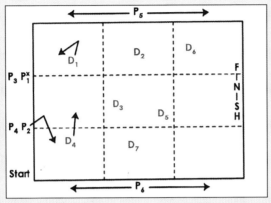

PRACTICE OUTCOMES

- To use stages of defence to limit attacking options and movement through the space.

- To be ball-side and marking a player in their area.

- To read others' intentions and be able to dictate and limit the options of attackers.

- To read and attend to relevant cues.

TASK/GROUP ORGANIZATION

Use a third of the court area and only two defenders in a channel/area at any one time.

Attackers in twos (Ps) move ball through the area, nearest D to P1 stage-three mark and D4 move to get ball-side of P2 and stop the front cut.

P1 and P2 can pass to each other, but can use the other Ps.

PROGRESSIONS AND DIFFERENTIATION

Attackers (P5 and P6 can move along line).

Defenders can double-mark in one channel.

POTENTIAL QUESTION TO POSE

What might the front defender do to outwit an attacker?

(Answer: Angle the body to see ball and player; be offline to disguise intention.)

that the player does not have the freedom to move to a desired location and will also force the player to a side line and into a crowded space. If a defender can restrict the attacker and keep the attacker away from ball side, the defender will force the opposition to use diagonal passes, which are more easily intercepted. If defenders are not successful at stage two, they must quickly recover and ensure that they close down the space.

Defenders must have good agility and use small running and shuffling steps to track and stay close to players in this stage. They should angle their body to drive the players away from the key attacking spaces. After stage two, defenders will be facing the player and not the ball, so it is vital that after momentarily delaying the run of the attacker they turn to face the ball.

Throughout each stage of defending, the player is striving to gain an interception and for this to occur a player must make a judgement as to the correct time to take-off for the intercept. Players should always seek opportunities to try for an interception and with good timing the frequency of a successful turnover will increase. The defender must also develop good vision in order to mark an opponent but also be aware of the path of the ball and

KEY COACHING POINTS FOR STAGE THREE DEFENCE

- Feet shoulder-width apart.
- Knees slightly flexed.
- Head and eyes up.
- Body angled to view player and the ball.
- Use stage one defending stance.

seek out an intercepting opportunity. This intercepting opportunity may require the player to drop off their own opponent and possibly move to another opponent or space. Deception on defence can trick the opposition into thinking that there is an attacking option not covered by the defender and by positioning away from the space and the opponent the defender makes a move for the interception.

A coach must plan to integrate technical netball skills in a session alongside game principles. Planning practices to develop techniques in simulated game contexts is an essential consideration for the coach in the youth context.

CHAPTER 6

COACHING DEFENSIVE SKILLS

Maggie Jackson

Each of the seven players on the court is required to defend and each must be able to demonstrate the ability to defend both on the receiver and on the ball. When marking the receiver the defender must shadow the attacker and restrict and prevent the attacker from moving into the desirable space. When defending on the ball a player can influence

Defending an opponent with the ball is important to apply pressure and to try and force a passing error. A defender must work hard to apply pressure to the shot.

the accuracy, direction, pace and height of the pass. By placing pressure on the ball the defender should limit the options by restricting the ball carrier's vision to locate the mover and passing space. In netball there are three stages of defence whereby a player makes attempts to gain an interception. When defending, a player should make a quick transition from one stage to the next, for example: one-on-one marking – pressure on the ball – restrict the player. At all times the player is trying to gain possession by forcing the receiver or ball carrier into an error.

All training and practice sessions for any age group must be planned to ensure they are fun, motivational and structured to develop the essential skills of the game. Practice must be purposeful at all times, with the coach setting specific goals to attain in each session. Any coach should strive to ensure an individual can perform effectively in competitive situations. Therefore the training session must expose young participants to game-like experiences as they develop their technical skills. Youth participants need to develop their understanding of defending in invasion games; it is important to note that some of the qualities required in netball can be found in other games too – for example, lacrosse, rugby, football, hockey and basketball. Sampling a range of sports at a young age will allow individuals to transfer some of the tactical aspects to netball.

Tactically, the above-mentioned games are similar even though the skills used are completely different. Six generic tactical tasks and abilities have been developed and they are applied here to defending in netball:

- Defending the goal.
- Keeping the ball away from the goal.
- Disrupting the attacking team's teamwork.
- Closing down the gaps.

- Preventing the effectiveness of feinting the ball or the feint by an attacking player.
- Limiting the options of the attacking players.

It is important for any player, at whatever age, to understand the game and be able to make decisions when under extreme pressure. A key reflection for coaches is for them to ask themselves whether a coaching session is designed to gain this experience. As a coach it is important to ensure the following aspects are incorporated: evidence of time pressure, high degrees of freedom, and high consequences for incorrect decisions made.

When a team is not in possession of

When defending, young players should learn to:

- Assess their opponents' speed and capabilities – for example, how fast are they? What do they do to get free? Do they prefer the left or the right side? Are they right- or left-handed? What is their most effective attacking move? Can they pass under pressure? Are they working in isolation?
- Assess whether they can intercept the ball – for example, are they in the most effective position? Is their opponent faster than them? Does the ball carrier have the ability to read their movement?
- Assess whether they can force the ball out of court – for example, force an error.
- Assess whether they can assist another defender to intercept the ball.

the ball all players become defenders, regardless of the bib they are wearing. This is an obvious statement, but how many players have been coached to think like that? When coaching the defensive demands of the game to youth participants we must ensure they develop to evaluate a range of actions.

To be an effective defender the young player must work hard to prevent the opposition scoring goals, create pressure at all times, and force the opposition to pass under pressure and create errors. In order to achieve these defensive actions the individual must practise being ball side and therefore in between the ball and the opponent. This should force a diagonal pass, putting the receiver under pressure and allowing a defender an opportunity to intercept. The young player can also strive to limit the number of shooting opportunities by encouraging the opposition to make more lateral passes or passes back before having an opportunity to score.

When designing a defensive session it is important for the participants to achieve success; it is therefore vital to ensure the space a group work in is not too large for a defender to cover. The smaller the space, the greater the level of success for a defending player. In addition it is useful to overload the team defending, so this could be a 4v3 practice where four players are in a defending role to ensure greater levels of success. All defending practices should be placed in a context of the game – for example, take the practice into a specific area: around the circle edge, from a loose ball situation, etc.

Defence Tasks

A young player must develop good body management and effective footwork skills. Youth participants must also recognize the importance of: (a) minimal contact, (b) prompting incorrect decisions by the ball carrier and/or the receiver, and (c) being able to change direction and/or elevate as quickly as possible. Attacking players move at varying speeds, change direction in a forward, backward, diagonal and sideways direction, jump and stop, so agility is critical if any defender is to be successful. A coach must ensure that defenders can be given the opportunity to practise and become aware of their strengths and what they need to improve upon.

When on defence, all players within the team need to:

- Show excellent fast footwork and agility.
- Understand where the least advantageous place is for their opponent to go to.
- Be able to change from attack to defence immediately.
- Be prepared to never give up.
- Be thinking all the time.
- Be prepared to take risks.
- Possess effective and wide-ranging vision.

A coach should also consider:

- How long the defender will work for.
- Is there a specific goal to reach?
- If quality of movement is the focus, work for shorter durations.

Here is an example of a task.

PURPOSE

To keep moving in and around the spots using a variety of foot patterns and ensuring the body continuously changes angle – for example, side steps, side slips, backwards, forwards, diagonal sprints, jumps off one and two feet. The defender must be able to see the ball all times.

PROGRESSIONS

a) Feeder holds the ball in one hand high, low, left and right and the defender must call out where the ball is.
b) Feeder passes the ball at random times.

ORGANIZATION

Pairs with one netball and six spots in half a third area.

Feeder holds ball on the third line and the spots are randomly scattered in the area.

QUESTIONS THAT CAN BE POSED

What direction is more natural for you? Which direction is harder? The response should demonstrate what participants are thinking, and show that they should practise what they find difficult.

GENERIC COACHING POINTS

Body upright; when static, be prepared with knees slight flexed; ensure players are on the balls of their feet; small steps with the initial step moving forward; as the ball is caught take an extra step so there is a feel of running through the catch; and when catching the ball take the ball 'off the line'.

Here are six addtional tasks.

PRACTICE I

PURPOSE

Both defenders work simultaneously to keep the balloons off the floor.

PROGRESSIONS OF THE TASK

a) Only use identified hand.
b) Reduce or increase the number of balloons.
c) Tip another pair's balloon and score a point – you might need to reduce the initial number of balloons used.

ORGANIZATION

Pairs with four balloons in a 3 × 4m space.

QUESTIONS THAT CAN BE POSED

How do you change direction when you are at full sprint speed to keep the balloon off the floor or to tip another pair? Response could be: keep upwards when sprinting, brake with the outside foot and immediately step onto the other foot.

GENERIC COACHING POINTS

Body upright; when static, be prepared with knees slight flexed; ensure players are on the balls of their feet; small steps with the initial step moving forward; as the ball is caught take an extra step so there is a feel of running through the catch; and when catching the ball take the ball 'off the line'.

PRACTICE 2

PURPOSE

'Defenders' working to cooperate and maintain a 'tennis' rally with their hands, always ensuring the ball bounces once only – how long a rally can you manage without it bouncing more than once or going outside the area?

PROGRESSIONS

a) Must only use the forehand.
b) The hit must alternate between a short, then long distance.
c) As in (b), widen the area.

ORGANIZATION

Pairs with one tennis ball in a 5 × 5 space.

QUESTIONS THAT CAN BE POSED

What movement do you find difficult to do and what movement slows you down so that changing direction becomes difficult?

PRACTICE 3

PURPOSE

One defender skips and the other defender joins in; they continue as a pair within the rope.

PROGRESSIONS

a) Different speeds of the rope.
b) 1-foot and 2-foot jumps.

ORGANIZATION

Pairs and a skipping rope.

QUESTIONS THAT CAN BE POSED

Can you consider different jumps and movement patterns and still be successful? The response could be: 1–2; 2–1; 2–2.

PRACTICE 4

PURPOSE

Two feeders pass the ball flat and chest height to each other approximately 2 metres apart and the defender stands to the side or behind one of the feeders and sprints in and catches the ball.

When the defender stands behind the feeder the footwork is as follows. When going around the right side of the feeder the defender moves the right foot away from the feeder and then immediately the left foot comes through near to the feeder (with no contact). The defender then sprints to catch the ball as far as possible away from the potential receiver.

PROGRESSIONS

a) Keep the task continuous for an identified time period with the defender passing the ball to one of the feeders; sprint to a specific point identified by the defender and then go in to catch the ball again.

b) As in (a) but now pass to the opposite feeder and still touch a point nearer than in (a) and amend the footwork patterns so you can change direction and possibly move backwards to catch the ball from the feeder.

ORGANIZATION

Three players and a netball.

QUESTIONS THAT CAN BE POSED

How far are you able to be from the feeder and still successfully sprint and catch the ball?

PRACTICE 5

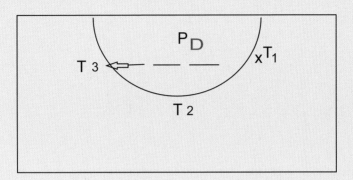

PURPOSE

Three static feeders stand around the circle edge (top, left and right) and the attacker is static in the circle and defender starts behind the attacker. T1, T2 and T3 pass the ball to each other. In the diagram T1 has the ball so the defender is placed in front of the player. The defender moves around the player so that she is able to be in an intercepting position without contacting.

PROGRESSIONS

a) Consider intercepting the pass between the feeders.
b) Feeders randomly pass into the static attacker.
c) The defender not only moves round the front of the attacker to be in the appropriate position but also moves around the back of the attacker to get into position.
d) The attacker changes angle.
e) Reduce the size of the working area and the attacker moves at a 50% work rate within the inner circle area.

ORGANIZATION

Three static throwers, one player and one defender and a ball in the defending circle.

QUESTIONS THAT CAN BE POSED

How can you put doubt in the mind of the feeder? Response could be: to move continuously around the opponent with the head up.

PRACTICE 6

PURPOSE

Feeder calls turn right or left and then passes the ball in different places around the defender. The defender must need to be able to move at least two or three steps to catch the ball. The defender returns to the starting point and turns away from the feeder. Repeat and continue for an identified time.

PROGRESSIONS

a) Reduce the time of calling the direction and passing the ball.

b) Increase the range and at the same time speed up the feeding so there has to be faster recovery by the defender.

c) Add the instructions right high or low/left high or low.

d) When the defender is returning to the starting point, pass a high ball at random points (not every time). This ensures the player returns to the starting point facing the ball before turning to start the task again.

ORGANIZATION

Pairs and a tennis ball or another type of ball. Feeder stands 2 metres away from the defender and the defender stands with his or her back to the feeder.

QUESTIONS THAT CAN BE POSED

Give me an example of how this practice applies to a game situation. Response could be: (a) assisting you with listening to instructions on the court, and (b) when you need to recover quickly on court to another position.

We obviously want to encourage young players to learn the fun and enjoyment of intercepting passes, and this is an important skill, but it is also vital to coach them to 'do their own job' first before looking for an interception. This involves trying to dominate and restrict the movement of their opponent. Defenders should work to dictate the space available to their opponents, forcing them towards the side or goal line, towards an area that could mean the opponent might go offside, towards another member of your own team or into a crowded area.

An opposing team is under pressure when they (a) are not able to pass the ball towards their attacking goal and have to make several lateral passes or passes going backwards, (b) are passing long diagonal passes with the ball receiver running away from the ball carrier, (c) are having to pass the ball along the same channel, and (d) can only deliver a high lofted pass.

The next four tasks focus on the interception.

A player must show determination in defence.

PRACTICE 7

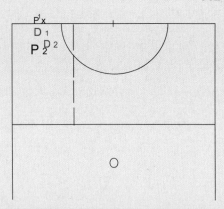

TASK AND POTENTIAL PROGRESSIONS

a) The attackers (P) must make at least a minimum of three passes before they can score a goal. The attackers are only permitted to make flat passes.
b) The attackers (P) must get ball side to receive a pass.
c) Free flow – allow the attackers to make their own choices.
d) Widen the court area to half the width of a court.

ADDITIONAL COACHING POINTS

Each defender must ensure that she 'does her own job' first. A range of options are open to a defender, such as: drop off onto another player, dictate the space and force an attacker to a line, force the attacker to make a short pass, force an opponent into another defender, step up to the attacker who passes the ball and dictate by angling the body where you want her to move, or lastly when the attacker has the ball the defender is 0.9 metres away and marking the pass.

ORGANIZATION

In fours; two defenders and two attackers and one ball. Start in width of a third of a third of the court.

The defenders are aiming to intercept or aiming to dictate the attackers (P) so they have to make numerous passes laterally/backwards. The attackers are aiming to catch the ball over the third line to score a goal. When the defenders intercept the pass or force a ball to go out of court they have scored a goal and the attackers have to start again on the base line.

QUESTIONS THAT CAN BE POSED

What will make you decide where to angle yourself when standing 3 feet away marking the ball? Response could be: by looking at the other near team members and where they are dictating their opponents.

GAME CONTEXT

This can be done from a dead ball situation, i.e. side lines, back lines and free passes.

PRACTICE 8

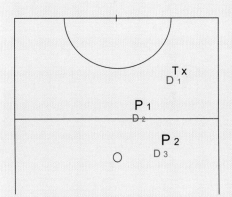

QUESTIONS THAT CAN BE POSED

Why are you marking the ball at that angle? Response could be that it is near a side line.

Where will you dictate the ball carrier once she passes the ball? Response could be: step in and dictate to prevent a forward pass.

If you jump when marking the ball what is the advantage and what do you need to be aware of? Response could be that the jump may tip/intercept the pass and the disadvantage could be that the ball carrier then slips through for a forward pass while the defender is in the air.

ORGANIZATION

In a group of six; three attackers and three defenders in half the width of a court in a third of the court and one ball.

TASK AND POTENTIAL PROGRESSIONS

a) TX stands, back to the goal, holding the ball and tosses the ball in the air, catches it and pivots to face the attacking goal. Defender 1 gets a 3-foot mark and marks the ball. The other P2 and D2 are set up approximately 3 metres away; D2 dictates the player into D1. P3 stands further away and moves to receive the first pass as D3 is forcing P3 to move in the forward direction. Defender 1 and 2 now 'do their own job' and dictate their opposing attackers into areas they do not want to go to, i.e. lines, short passes but not long straight ball side passes. Every time the attacker catches the pass the opposing defender must mark the ball. Can the defender force an error? Can the defender intercept the pass?

b) As above, but now try marking the ball by (a) leaning, (b) leaning and then jumping. Consider what is the most effective.

c) As in (a) but doing their own job, but now are the defenders aware that they can intercept a pass off attacker 3?

GAME CONTEXT

Back line pass, side line pass and free passes.

PRACTICE 9

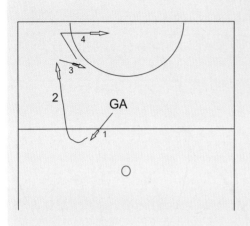

PURPOSE

Ask the players to consider the movement of what (a) a Goal Attack would like to do at the centre pass; (b) a Goal Shooter would like to do if she comes out of the circle to receive a pass; (c) a Goal Defence would like to do at a centre pass.

What would then be your movement to dictate their movements? What kind of foot-work would you use?

The diagram shows four consecutive potential movements from a centre pass. It demon-strates the GA sprinting out to receive a potential centre pass (1), then sprinting down towards the circle (2), attempting to enter the top of the circle (3), but then moving and entering along the base line (4).

Example of possible footwork to use to dictate the Goal Attack by the defender: sprint, stage 2 marking, then stepping in and open out body so player is on your back; side slipping or side step-ping, turn to face player to stop player entering the circle, open out and track along base line, sprint diagonally forward to intercept the 'ball'.

The diagram of possible movements by the GS demonstrates the first movement out of the circle (1), and then back towards the circle (2), around the circle edge and in through the top of the circle (3).

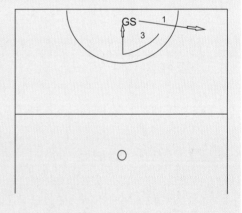

Example of possible footwork to use to dictate the Goal Shooter: sprint, small steps backwards, and then step in to opponent to prevent entry back into the circle, side steps to dictate the player away from the base line, open out to get opponent onto the back of the defender, turn again and then turn again with opponent onto the back and side step to keep shooter at the circle edge, sprint to intercept 'ball' at the top of the circle.

PRACTICE 9 (continued)

The diagram of the possible movement by the GD demonstrates the GD getting free to be a possible receiver of the centre pass (1), sprints towards the side line taking the GD (2), and then a possible receiver in the centre third (3).

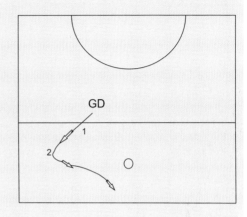

Example of possible footwork to track and dictate the Goal Defence: two steps sprint, turn to face the opponent, side step to prevent forward movement and dictate to the side line, open out and side step or side slipping to keep opponent on the back, turn to continue to prevent opponent moving up the court, open out again to get opponent on the back and then sprint/sideslip and jump to intercept the 'ball'.

ORGANIZATION

Working on own and no ball required.

QUESTIONS THAT CAN BE POSED

What is the cue that makes you get your opponent on your back? Response could be: when the opponent has started to go ahead of your leading shoulder and by opening out you are dictating the opponent's movement again.

Why is it advantageous to get your opponent on your back? Response could be: you can see the ball and more players.

What is the cue that then makes you turn again to face your opponent? Response could be: the opponent has changed direction again and you can dictate the opponent again.

What other situations could we consider? Response could be: a centre taking a side line throw-in in the attacking third.

PRACTICE 10

TASK AND POTENTIAL PROGRESSIONS

a) Attacker is only allowed to initially move forward or back. Defender is focusing on dictating the attacker towards the attacker's goal and putting pressure on the attacker so that she can only receive overhead balls near the back line.

b) The task is repeated, dictating towards the feeder, so only front short passes (use a smaller area to start with).

c) The feeder is able to pass to the other feeder – the defender must dictate to the back and not let the attacker cross the dotted line. The defender is therefore continuing to dictate (trying to position the attacker) wide to the back line.

d) As (c) but dictating forward.

e) Attacker speeds up movement.

GAME CONTEXT

Set up the practice as a back line pass: Goal Keeper, Goal Defence, Wing Defence (Centre if High 5s). Opposing Goal Attack on attacking Goal Defence.

Goal Attack is dictating for the Goal Defence to receive a forward short first pass from the Goal Keeper. The Goal Keeper passes the first pass to the Wing Defence (centre in High 5s). The Goal Attack must dictate the Goal Defence to not receive a forward pass towards the attacking goal.

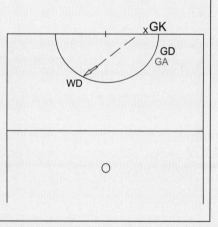

ORGANIZATION

Two feeders, one attacker and one defender and one ball in the size of a third of a third of court.

QUESTIONS THAT CAN BE POSED

How do you ensure you are dictating a short pass but not contacting? Response could be: keeping the feet moving and the body upright.

Where in the game can you dictate only a long overhead pass? Response could be: towards the base line.

How Do We Coach and Develop a Relentless Approach?

The qualities of defenders are often described as risk takers, relentless, proactive, determined and courageous. These qualities are not always innate and coaching sessions need to be planned so they can be developed and practised. Youth participants do not often like being in close proximity to others, so asking a defender to step in and restrict and domi-nate the movements of an opponent might be alien to some and needs practice. Defenders must be able to problem-solve and find accurate solutions as they cannot rely on the coach when in the competitive game context. Defenders who are trying to sprint and take interceptions but miss on numerous situations must not be discouraged while they are practising this skill. The next two tasks offer examples.

The arms of a player over the ball can force a lofted pass, which may be intercepted by another defender. Forcing a diagonal pass is an aim of any team on defence.

PRACTICE II

ORGANIZATION

Eight players (four defenders and four attackers).

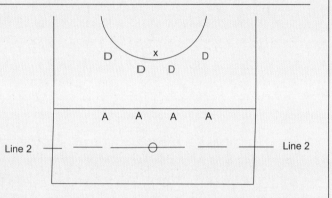

The ball is placed on the circle edge.

The four attackers run and move around the defenders to pick up the ball. The defenders merely dictate, deny and track the attacking players (no contact). As soon as the ball is picked up the defenders need to move into dominant positions to slow down the attacking team and possibly intercept the pass.

The attacking team need to access the ball and then score by catching the ball over line 2. If the defenders force the error or gain the interception they score a point and the attacking team restart just into the centre third.

GAME CONTEXT

This practice can be related to the speed of transition from attack to defence and identify where all defenders need to get round the attacking players and restrict their movement up the court so that the attacking team can only pass laterally or backwards.

QUESTIONS THAT CAN BE POSED

When tracking and restricting the movement of the attackers away from the ball, where are you trying to force them to go?

Do you step up or let the attackers come to you and for what reason? The response could be: step up.

When the attacking team gets the ball, what must the defending team do? The response could be: immediately get around to force the players with the ball away from their target goal.

PRACTICE 12

CONTINUOUS END BALL

Eight players in half a court; four defenders and four attackers. The aim is for both teams to score in a netball goal when they are on the attack. Only two attackers and two defenders are allowed in the circle at any one time (this can vary).

If the attacking team score, they keep the ball and have to attack back to the half way point and then attack again. If they rebound from a missed shot they have to attack back to the centre third and start again.

If the defence force an error or gain an interception or gain rebound from a goal, the defenders change to attackers and the attackers change to defenders and they pass the ball back to the centre third and then they attack towards the goal.

The game needs to be played for a set time or a set number of goals.
Conditions can be set up as an attacking team such as (a) having to pass the ball out of the circle once it is in the attacking circle and then the ball can be passed into the circle and a shot can be tried, (b) the attacking team have to pass the ball back to the centre third when it enters the end third before a shot can be tried.

QUESTIONS THAT CAN BE POSED

As a defender where are you wishing the attackers to put shots up? Response could be: the outer areas of the circle.

How are you going to win the rebound in the circle as a defender? Response could be: to step in and turn to see the ball following the attempt at shot.

Are you considering whether you are dictating your attacking players together or apart?

Defending can be great fun and when performed effectively can change and uplift the game. For youth participants it is essential that the whole team are given the time in training to be coached defensive play so that the skills and the understanding of the game become embedded in their performances. It is important to allow young players the freedom to experiment with a range of movements and tactics so as to promote innovative actions by the individual player. Consequently, by considering the design and relevance of the task, the amount of feedback and appropriate questions, the participant can begin to understand the defensive game.

CHAPTER 7

TOP PRACTICES FOR DEVELOPING ATTACKING SKILLS

Denise Egan

Coaching is a process that commits to developing the whole person, endeavouring to nurture not only the technical and tactical but the social, emotional and psychological components. Adopting the notion of the five Cs as covered in this text will enable young people in netball to achieve within this supportive and nurturing climate. Young participants require the coach to understand them as individuals, while acknowledging that everyone is different and will develop at different rates. A young participant may be physically mature for their age but may not have the same level of emotional maturity. Coaching should be positive, and encouragement is essential to support young people to make the most of

A modified game-like practice is effective for learning.

their abilities, knowing there will be many variations in individual capacities within a session.

The practice design techniques and strategies adopted by a coach are critical in ensuring that there is an opportunity for the young participant to develop holistically. Offering practices with choice, collaboration and opportunity for an individual to think creatively will serve to provide a suitable motivational climate for learning and retention of skills and understanding. Coaches must ensure they do not place a so-called 'ceiling effect' on a practice by directing a young participant to the desired action and by structuring the practice so there is only one choice, hence no decision to be made. The need for a random and/or variable practice design is therefore an essential part of a coaching tool kit.

Random practice will incorporate more than one technical skill per practice and is often referred to as a 'smart combination' practice design. In a random practice structure participants will be challenged to select the appropriate skill for the context which they are experiencing. For example, if an opponent is faster than the player is, the choice of a change of direction to get free would be a more useful action than trying to sprint in one direction to get free.

Variable practice will incorporate one skill but will involve a changing environment and context so as to prompt decision-making. Variable practices are often referred to as 'smart variations'. In a variable practice the participant will be faced with a changing context and so is faced with executing a skill in different conditions. For example, the participant may be executing a shoulder pass but be faced with the need to vary the pace and timing of the pass given the defensive positioning of the opponents. In addition, the receiver may be moving towards or away from the ball carrier so the timing of the release point may change.

When young people are working in groups, many tasks and activities are suited to grid-style spaces and small group sizes. A coach should try not to overuse spot markers to identify the working area but begin to develop players' awareness of the space they are working within. Small group sizes are encouraged for young participants, as there will be greater activity time and fewer communication channels, so a collaborative environment can gradually be developed. More participants in a group will demand a greater level of communication and this should be a progressive challenge for the individual. When increasing the group sizes it is best practice to select numbers to make it easier to progress. A coach must also be aware of the progression and the level of social interaction amongst the groups. It is easy to go from 2s to 4s to 6 or 8s and also 1s to 3s to 6s.

Children between the ages of six to eight or nine years of age should enjoy a wide range of movement activities within a practice and session, and opportunities for creativity should be offered. Between the ages of eight to twelve years, individual technical skills and mastery are recommended with high levels of discovery-based learning. At this age elements of formal competition should be introduced where approximately 25 per cent of the training will focus on fitness.

Teenagers between the ages of eleven and sixteen will also require high levels of support for the development of training, but coaches should group on biological maturity rather than chronological and be aware of growth spurts. Participants will strive to win, but an emphasis on performance is still crucial at this age as well as gaining learning from competitive experiences. Connection and confidence will often dip during puberty, and the coach should be mindful of grouping strategies when planning sessions as friendship groups may be more suitable.

The following section will overview the 5Cs of importance when planning and delivering a practice with young participants. After a review of the 5Cs the chapter will present ten practices that will help develop attacking skills in the young participant.

For a practice to be effective in promoting the all-round development of a young participant the coach must be mindful of the Cs. The Cs promote the development of competence, confidence, character, and connection. In this chapter the need to plan a practice considering a fifth C of creativity is integrated.

Competence is where skills are developed appropriately at the correct time of an individual's development. The netball coach should carefully plan activities to include the physical, technical, social, personal, tactical and psychological performance competencies.

Confidence should be considered and enhanced through a practice. The coach will provide positive feedback and support the child in developing strategies to cope with mistakes and setbacks as part of this process. Confidence is an internal intrinsic value and relates to adopting a 'can do' attitude. A young participant must be exposed to success, to realistic individual and group challenges in order to develop resilience to cope with both success and difficulties encountered. An environment has to be developed by the netball coach that stresses the value of personal improvement with an emphasis on effort and perseverance to gain improvement in performance.

Character should be developed through the coach, creating an environment where respect for all participants, officials, parents, coaches and the rules of netball is a core value adopted by all involved. Participants need to

Setting a practice that encourages creativity and decision-making is essential to develop the netball player.

be able to develop standards for their own behaviours in a session, in society and within a range of cultures to gain a sense of right and wrong. Caring for others in sport is associated with developing sympathy and empathy, where the recognition of the strengths and limitations of oneself and team-mates is accepted and appreciated.

Creativity. The children's coach has to be able to encourage participants to find solutions to problems themselves through discovery, trial and error and problem-solving tasks. Young people must be set scenarios or tasks where they have to think for themselves and understand how things work rather than copy and repeat.

Connection is concerned with the importance of being part of a group and being able to build relationships with individuals, institutions, teams and clubs. Connection is the ability to work with and help others as an individual or in a group.

The above details should be at the forefront of a coach's mind-set when planning practices for a youth session in netball. Some considerations for coaching youth participants are summarized below:

SOME CONSIDERATIONS

- Play to the rules.
- Match young people carefully (both physically and on ability).
- Use grids with enough space between groups.
- Use appropriate equipment (for example, a size 4 rather than size 5).
- Check that young people play with sensible challenge (contact) and have vision when moving into space.
- Praise effort and improvement or progress with less emphasis on winning.

The following ten practices offer the coach an opportunity to address the 5Cs and focus on attacking skills. The key below relates to all ten practices.

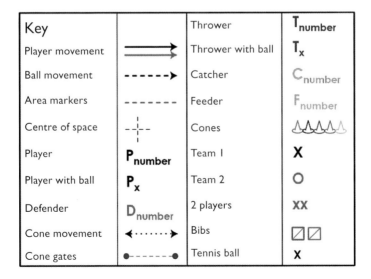

Key		Thrower	T_{number}
Player movement	⟶	Thrower with ball	T_x
Ball movement	- - - -▶	Catcher	C_{number}
Area markers	- - - - - -	Feeder	F_{number}
Centre of space	- -╎- -	Cones	ᐃᐃᐃᐃᐃ
Player	P_{number}	Team 1	X
Player with ball	P_x	Team 2	O
Defender	D_{number}	2 players	XX
Cone movement	◀ ······ ▶	Bibs	▨▨
Cone gates	●- - - - -●	Tennis ball	X

PRACTICE I: BALL SKILLS – PASS, CATCH AND SEE

Six participants. Two ball square – attacker is receiving the ball from a player after moving to a cone and must send the ball to a free player who is static on the perimeter.

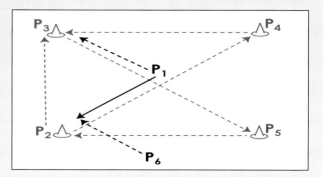

PRACTICE OUTCOMES

To pass the ball flat and fast.

To pass the ball on a 1 and 2 second release.

To use peripheral vision to sight a free player to whom to pass.

To pass the ball ahead of the moving player.

ORGANIZATION

Players 2, 3, 4 and 5 are static and will be passing a ball between them.

P1 moves to a cone and receives a pass from P6.

P1 must then pass the ball to P2, 3, 4 or 5, who is not in possession of the other ball or about to receive a pass.

The player who received the pass from P1 sends it back to P6 (repeat).

Work for 45 seconds.

HOW TO DEVELOP THE 5CS IN THIS PRACTICE

Competence   P6 to vary the type of pass used, chest, bounce, overhead, shoulder, underarm etc. P1 must use a different type of pass to the one they received from P6. Reminder of the 3-second rule for the ball carrier.

Connection   Work to sight others and pick up cues from individuals (see the position of ball carrier's body and holding position of the ball). Encourage worker P1 to call out the name of the person who caught the other ball.

Character and Caring   Find solutions to problems addressing the quick release and speed of ball.

Confidence   Praise quick decision-making and acknowledge the difficulty of the practice (praise work rate and effort). Support and reassure when dealing with mistakes or frustration.

Creativity   Experiment to find solutions – ball may be released into space/loose ball for P1 to retrieve.

PRACTICE 2: BALL SKILLS – ATTACK THE COLOUR

Two participants. Players work on their capacity to process information moving at speed to receive the ball.

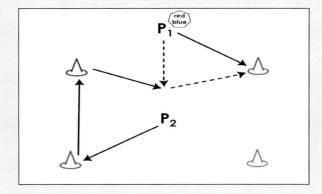

PRACTICE OUTCOMES

To use sprint and change of direction.

To pass ahead of receiver in the space.

Pass the ball flat and fast.

Move onto the ball at speed.

Use a range of passing options

ORGANIZATION

Four spot markers and players work in half of a third area.

PI calls two colours and P2 must move to both cones before receiving a pass from PI in the centre.

PI must then move to receive a pass at one of the other coloured cones not called by P2 (in this example PI moves to green).

Practice restarts with PI at green.

HOW TO DEVELOP THE 5CS IN THIS PRACTICE

Competence Change of direction and attacking sprint movement. Ability to process information – memory. Physical effort for anaerobic sprinting movement.

Connection Learning to work with others one to one and accuracy of passing. Becoming self-aware of ability to develop basic skill and decision-making.

Character and Caring Respect footwork rule and ensure the worker has success on the final ball into the middle space.

Confidence Aim to set target of effective movement and quick decision-making and strive to retrieve loose balls (resilience).

Creativity Increase the problem by changing the distribution of the markers/colour pattern.

PRACTICE 3: CATCH, CONTEST AND DELIVER

Four participants. High passing technique combined with elevation and take-off from one to two feet.

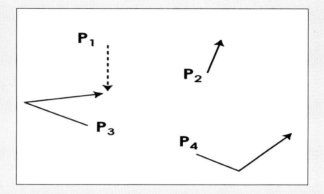

PRACTICE OUTCOMES

To use a one/two handed catch when receiving a high pass.

To use full arm extension to catch the pass as early as possible.

To execute a pass into the air/space above the receiver.

To pass a high ball to moving players.

ORGANIZATION

PI to P4 pass a ball in an area.

Players must first lead away from the ball carrier and then receive a high pass on second lead.

All three players offer for a pass and the ball carrier selects one to pass to.

Ball carrier can bounce ball firmly onto ground for high ball for quick reaction.

HOW TO DEVELOP THE 5CS IN THIS PRACTICE

Competence Take off technique is developed from one or two feet. Timing of the jump to receive a high ball. Ball placement into air (accuracy of extension of release). Mental control of emotion on contest for ball.

Connection Understanding of rule to contest – body alignment. Gaining advantage by technical and physical aspects but abiding to rule – no contact.

Character and Caring When to contest fairly and appropriately with sense of right and wrong – no rough unfair contest. Going for ball but mindful of others.

Confidence 'My ball' attitude, coping with loss and gain of ball. Learning to elevate from one or a two-footed stance.

Creativity Use balloons, variety of sizes and colours, so players have to tip in the air or tap out or into area away from other attackers.

PRACTICE 4: PASS, INTERCHANGE AND SWITCH

Four participants. Players pass and move in the space and on coach call will interchange to work with a player from other pairing.

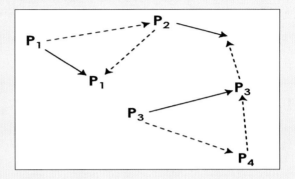

PRACTICE OUTCOMES

To use a range of passing techniques while moving at speed.

To balance the practice area with the other pair working in the space.

To execute a fast catch and quick release action.

Applying the footwork rule for land step and throw action.

ORGANIZATION

Four players working in pairs in half of third area and one ball between two players.

Players pass and move around in the area/space and must pass to a moving player.

On a Coach call of 'change' or 'switch' the players not in possession of a ball must switch with the other partner.

Players should work for 45 seconds.

HOW TO DEVELOP THE 5CS IN THIS PRACTICE

Competence   Technical ability to choose correct movement and type of pass to use. Decision-making will be around the focus of attention. Coach could ask to see short and long passes.

Connection   Making switch with others in safe and fun manner without causing contact or breaking any rules on footwork, passing and catching. Working with all players to keep possession. Key target/goal 10–20 passes.

Character and Caring   Avoiding the space of others. Having empathy for non-ball carrier when changing partners (ball safety). Linking with others to ensure easy catching of ball into space.

Confidence   Promote passing, moving and throwing technique in crowded space – add more pairs into grid. Challenge by goal setting and gain communication both verbal and visual on switching.

Creativity   Could ask for five switches then ball carrier moves into another grid.

PRACTICE 5: RESPONSE SELECTION – CONFUSION

Three participants. Players work on their capacity to process information and move at speed to receive the ball while being defended in the space.

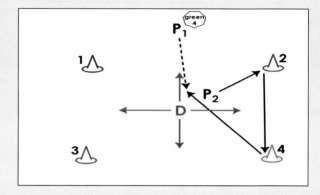

PRACTICE OUTCOMES

To maintain speed of movement under cognitive pressure.

To execute a change of direction or sliding/shuffling movement.

To use a range of movement skills to outwit the defender in the centre space.

To learn the strengths and weaknesses of each defender.

ORGANIZATION

Four coloured cones (soft touch) and players work in half a third.

Each cone has number with PI calling colour and a number to which P2 reacts quickly and moves to or around the cone.

The ball is passed into the centre space where defender is covering (space to be defined).

After six repetitions PI and P2 and defender change roles

HOW TO DEVELOP THE 5CS IN THIS PRACTICE

Competence Change of pace and direction, reading defender, thinking and moving, passing to attacker when defended. Get ball side attacker/defender. Call three colours/numbers, e.g. one red and two.

Connection Build relationship with ball carrier. Defenders working within rules of contest, contact and 0.9m marking of the ball carrier.

Character and Caring Changing roles so that all participants get equal practice to achieve success. Set goal to improve ability to get ball side and not go behind the defender.

Confidence Command high work rate (physical) of self and learn different attacking movements versus different defenders. Keep going when defender achieving success.

Creativity Working out how best to get free after increased temporal loading and physical effort. Use feigning or fake of ball or head or body parts

PRACTICE 6: FREE SPACE AND VISION

Four participants. Four players move within an area that has five spaces defined.

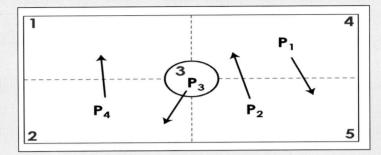

PRACTICE OUTCOMES

To use vision to move into a free space changing pace and direction.

To use peripheral vision and read off the front player to locate next available space.

Add defenders to two areas to track attackers.

ORGANIZATION

Use third of court.

Define the area into five spaces- or ensure there is always one more space in relation to number of players in the area.

Players can only stay in an area for up to 3 seconds.

Work for 30–60 seconds.

HOW TO DEVELOP THE 5CS IN THIS PRACTICE

Competence Vision and the ability to read off other players, use change of pace and direction. Develop spatial awareness.

Connection Be able to change direction when another person is moving into the same space as you.

Character and Caring Be aware of the 3-second rule in an area, respect that you might have to change your mind when two people enter an area at the same time – concede to others and create space.

Confidence Teamwork and avoiding the space of others. When defenders are added to two areas aim to track and delay the attackers. Show determination to outwit them with a change of pace or direction.

Creativity Add a ball for the attackers, set goal of all attackers to receive in each area or number of passes but all attackers must receive a pass at least once etc. Let participants decide on goal/target. Use a range of balls, e.g. tennis, basketball, football, rugby ball.

PRACTICE 7: BREAK, SPRINT AND TOUCH

Each player must touch the centre of each line defining their space with a defender restricting the movement.

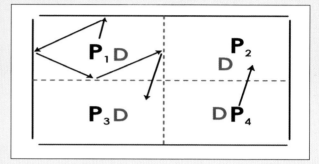

PRACTICE OUTCOMES

To work on the sprint and change of direction to get free.

Defender to try and angle their body so that the attacker has to work around them.

Defender and attackers must build up mental picture of which lines have been touched

ORGANIZATION

Eight players maximum per third.

Each player must touch the centre point of each line before moving into the next area clockwise.

Two attacking players could be working in one area at the same time.

The defender restricts the movement of the attacker to the line for a period of 3 seconds.

HOW TO DEVELOP THE 5CS IN THIS PRACTICE

Competence Gaining a high level of success in each area against various defenders. Develop improved performance in sprint and the change of direction, pace.

Connection Add players to the outside area who can team tag with attackers or defenders and enter area/swap over. Work as a team.

Character and Caring Building goals and targets that are realistic but challenge each individual.

Confidence Score points by touching eight lines then become a tagger/defender. Make decisions based on others.

Creativity Finding solutions and discovering how to beat each defender with which type of movement. If defender touches attacker the attacker, then has to go out of the area and re-enter another area. Introduce coloured spots and have to touch different colours as called by coach.

PRACTICE 8: TRANSITION TEAM CHALLENGE

Eight participants. Team challenge in which both teams pass and move, with a team making the transition to defend the other team if their colour is called.

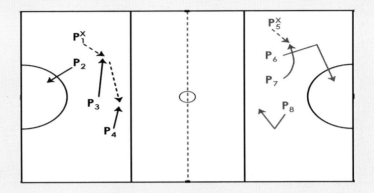

PRACTICE OUTCOMES

To execute an effective transition from attack to defence.

To devise strategies to counteract the defending team.

The attacking team must describe the strategies used by the defence to try and counteract their play.

ORGANIZATION

4 v 4 with bibs and work for 30–60 seconds, passing a ball in each area.

Coach calls colour of bibs and this team defend- they pass their ball to coach.

The attacking team must receive ball over the middle line.

Eight spot markers can be placed at the half way point and when the team scores they put marker on goal line.

HOW TO DEVELOP THE 5CS IN THIS PRACTICE

Competence Ensure that each attacking team have three offers for the ball carrier that are long, mid and short distances with breadth and depth to split the defenders.

Connection Working with others to devise strategies to attack and recognize defender tactics. Discussion and thinking as a team. Using rules of 3 seconds with ball carriers and non-contact as well as the 0.9m marking rule.

Character and Caring Catching and throwing and moving while under pressure and the ability to cope with a transition from possession to non-possession. Supporting each other in attack.

Confidence Learning to work with others and develop communication skills to bond as a team. Gaining success from persistence.

Creativity Add variety of different balls. Each team to take their ball to a goalpost so both balls working through the court.

PRACTICE 9: CONTROL THE PRESSURE

Two to eight participants. Attackers must pass ball as the number of defenders gradually increases against them in the space.

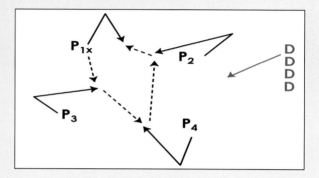

PRACTICE OUTCOMES

To use a range of methods to get free from the defenders.

To make the correct decision of who to offload the ball to.

To pass ball-side of the defender.

To use clearing moves and re-offer to open up space for oneself and others.

To ensure there are two offers for the ball carrier.

ORGANIZATION

Work in half a third area.

Attackers must pass the ball without defenders for 3–7 passes (coach select) then one defender moves into area and attackers pass another 3–7 passes, etc.

Attackers aim to complete 3–5 sets can have 2 v 2, 3v3, 4v4 etc.

The attacking team can have a 'chance' at each stage (2v1, 2v2 or 3v1 3v2 etc.).

Progress by attackers having to touch a line before offering to receive a pass.

HOW TO DEVELOP THE 5CS IN THIS PRACTICE

Competence Pass and move in small space working with others and develop decision making of spatial concepts.

Connection Gaining knowledge of attackers and defenders strengths and weaknesses and working together to build on strengths of individuals.

Character and Caring Coping with failure when defenders can enter all at the same time. Being resilient to keep offering when space is limited.

Confidence Control of body and mind when pressure builds up.

Creativity Take ball to goal if successful at all stages. Go out of the area to create space. Use variety of fakes and stepping actions to disguise intention in attack

PRACTICE 10: PASS AND CLEAR

Two to eight participants. Attackers must pass ball as the number of defenders gradually increases against them in the space.

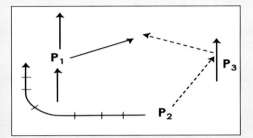

PRACTICE OUTCOMES

To use a single lead at speed to receive the ball.

To move toward the ball carrier when receiving the pass.

To balance the court/area using the three channels.

To move the ball through the court with control, balance and use of footwork rule.

To pass the ball accurately to a moving player.

ORGANIZATION

Work in half a third area.

Use a quarter of the netball court from goal line to half way or increase to two or three thirds.

Three groups allocated to work up and down in the space.

Players should pass the ball to each other working to keep the ball flat and fast and move behind the player they passed the ball to.

Or they could pass and go away from person who received the ball to fill in channel left free.

Create a 3 v 2 situation with a defender on 1 v 1 defence.

HOW TO DEVELOP THE 5CS IN THIS PRACTICE

Competence Experience working with others to develop skills of passing and receiving to moving players. Developing control over speed and balance to be able to execute accurate passing.

Connection Helping individuals to develop movement and decision-making skills, working to penetrate the forward space.

Character and Caring Recognizing the strengths and limitations of others both in physical and technical ability to: catch, control the ball and body while working at speed. Applying the footwork and passing rules.

Confidence Improving skills of passing on the move while working on all channels of the area/court..

Creativity Add a reactive pass that will extend the players and enable them to have quick recovery to catch unexpected passes. Use variety of quick change to bring the practice the other way up and down the court. Add a defender to a channel.

CHAPTER 8

INTEGRATING THE RULES OF NETBALL IN A COACHING SESSION
Gary Burgess

When coaching children, a knowledge and understanding of the rules can lead to a better understanding of netball skills. Raising an awareness of the rules and introducing them early throughout coaching sessions will mean that players are conscious of what they can and cannot do as well as where they can and cannot go. Netball is a game with many complex rules that can often confuse young and new participants to the game, so it is important that coaches simplify them. The footwork rule, defending, 'obstruction' and 'contact' are all key to the development of skills, with other rules added when skills are developed and embedded.

A coach should continue to develop player understanding of the rules.

It is important that coaches use the correct terms from the rule book when coaching, as this will support young players when they play games with umpires. Statements such as 'you are too close', 'you took too many steps' or 'you are not allowed in that area' are not advisable and can be replaced with 'you are obstructing', 'you broke the footwork rule' or 'you are offside'.

Coaches should also ensure their players know the difference between minor and major infringements. Minor infringements are penalized with a free pass. These include footwork, offside, held ball (three seconds), replaying/repossession, and so on. The free pass is taken by a member of the opposing team, in the same place where the infringement occurred but the offending player is 'free' to move. Major infringements are penalized with a penalty pass. Players who commit major infringements must stand out of play in the position where the infringement occurred and cannot move until the ball has been passed. These include obstruction, contact and issues of player discipline.

The first rules that need to be mastered in order to aid the learning of core skills are footwork, the playing areas and the position of players for the start of play.

Footwork

Movement around the court is often one of the toughest challenges for young players. Many of the sports and games they play in school involve running freely without having to think too much about which foot they take off from, landed on or exactly how many steps they have taken. A player may receive the ball with one foot grounded, or jump to catch a ball and land on one foot. They can then choose to:

- Step with the other foot in any direction any number of times, pivoting on the landing foot.
- Jump from the landing foot onto the other foot.
- Step with the other foot and jump but must throw the ball or shoot before re-grounding either foot.

In addition to these actions a player may also receive the ball while both feet are grounded. They can also jump to catch a ball and land on two feet simultaneously. The player may choose to move either foot, and the remaining foot shall be considered to be the landing foot. All rules regarding the landing foot will then apply. Players, however, are not permitted to hop or drag their landing foot.

The young player should be encouraged to umpire small-sided games.

When judging if a player has broken the footwork rule, umpires will count the steps taken. If they count to three then the footwork rule has been broken. In the early stages of coaching, players can be encouraged to count the steps they have taken either out loud or in their head. Some coaches have found that asking players to pull one of their socks up so they have one long sock and one short sock can help players think about their footwork and remember which foot was their landing foot. Alternatively players can say different words relating to their left and right feet when they take steps, such as hot and chocolate, pop and corn, ice and cream, and so on.

PRACTICE: FOOTWORK 'HOPSCOTCH'

Players stand in a line and practise hopping from one foot to two feet, counting the steps out loud or in their head. This can be done in a relay or against another group. This practice can be progressed with a ball and feeder, where players try to ensure they take possession of the ball on one foot, step forward onto the other foot and then pass the ball. Alternatively they can jump, take possession of the ball, land on both feet simultaneously and step forward onto either foot and then pass the ball back to the feeder.

Once this has become embedded the coach can introduce the rules regarding the landing foot and dragging. As long as players keep their landing foot on the ground they can take as many steps in any direction with the other foot. This pivoting action on the land-ing foot can allow players to rotate through 360 degrees on their landing foot to find the next passing option. When pivoting on the landing foot, players must keep their foot in one place and it cannot be dragged on the court.

STICKY FOOT

Set up five players in a circle with a sixth player in the centre. One of the outside players feeds the ball to the player in the centre, who takes possession on one foot. This foot is now regarded as the sticky foot. The centre player steps forward onto the second foot, pivots on the landing/ sticky foot and passes the ball to a different player. Players should take care to ensure they pivot on a fixed point and that they do not drag the landing/sticky foot. They can also alternate the foot that they pivot on. Each player should take a turn in the middle.

Playing Areas and Position at the Start of Play

Coaching players where they can and cannot go and where they should stand at the start of play is critical for the game to function. Players should be coached from an early age that if they go into an area where they are not permitted they are deemed 'offside' and their team loses possession of the ball.

Coaches should educate players as to the finer points of the rules and expectations at the centre pass. All players must start in their playing areas and return to these imme-diately after a goal has been scored. Players need to wait for the whistle to be blown

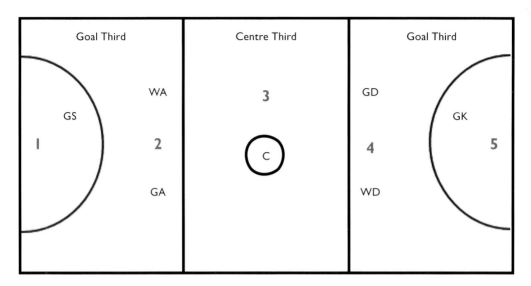

Goal Shooter	GS	Areas 1, 2
Goal Attack	GA	Areas 1, 2, 3
Wing Attack	WA	Areas 2, 3
Centre	C	Areas 2, 3, 4
Wing Defence	WD	Areas 3, 4
Goal Defence	GD	Areas 3, 4, 5
Goal Keeper	GK	Areas 4, 5

Fig. 8.1
Diagram of
playing areas.

before they enter the centre third. Immediately the whistle is blown, the waiting players are allowed into the centre third and the ball must be touched or caught in this third. An attacking centre has a specific task at a centre pass and must ensure that they are wholly within the centre circle ready for the whistle to be blown. This means that they should have at least one foot completely inside the circle at the point at which the whistle is blown.

Within the game there are other rules that young players will need to master in order for the game to function. These include:

- Playing the ball
- Scoring a goal
- Obstruction
- Contact

Playing the Ball

The 'playing the ball' rule states the actions players can perform to gain possession and what they can and cannot do when they have possession of the ball.

To gain possession players can:

- Bounce the ball once to gain possession.
- Roll the ball to themselves.

When in possession of the ball, players:

- Can pass or bounce the ball to another player.
- Must throw the ball within three seconds.

When in possession of the ball, players cannot:

- Bounce the ball more than once.
- Deliberately kick the ball.
- Hand or roll the ball to another player.
- Use the goal post as support.
- Place their hands on a ball held by an opponent.
- Throw the ball while sitting, lying or kneeling on the ground.
- Throw the ball over a complete third.
- Regain possession of the ball, having dropped or thrown it, before it has been touched by another player.

In addition to these rules, coaches should consider the 'short pass' and 'over a third' rules. A short pass infringement occurs when at the point a pass is made there is not enough room for a third player to pass between the hands of the thrower and the receiver. This infringement is penalized with a free pass in the position where the infringement occurred and the penalized player is free to move. An 'over a third' infringement occurs when the ball is thrown over one complete third of the netball court without being touched or caught by a player. This includes from one goal third to another and from a goal line throw-in into the centre third. This infringement is also penalized with a free pass and is

set in the third the ball was thrown to in line with where the ball crossed the transverse line. The player who caused the infringement is allowed to move. It is always beneficial for coaches to show young players these scenarios, as they are far more effective than a written or spoken description.

Scoring a Goal

The process of scoring a goal seems relatively straightforward; however, coaches should make it clear that there are certain things players can and cannot do. When taking a shot a player must be wholly within the goal circle, which means having no contact with the ground outside the circle or the line. One or both feet must also have had contact with the ground inside the goal circle. The player must complete a shot at goal within 3 seconds while observing the footwork rule. If a player breaks any of these rules a free pass is awarded to the opposition at the point at which the infringement occurred. In addition, players may not use the post to balance or to stop themselves from going out of court. This infringement is also penalized with a free pass to the opposition at the point at which the infringement occurred.

Coaches should be mindful that younger players may attempt a shot that misses the goal ring, the net or the goal post completely. The player who took the shot will be penalized for repossession if touching the ball before another player does, so it would be advisable to run through this scenario.

Obstruction

A defending player may attempt to defend from a distance of 0.9 metres from a player in possession of the ball. When coaching

The umpire will indicate using her arm which team have the centre pass after a goal is scored.

'obstruction' it is useful to have a metre stick or a 0.9 metre measure, as it gives the players a tangible idea of what 0.9 metres looks like. Alternatively, the centre circle on court is typically 0.9 metres in diameter.

As players become more skilled, coaches can introduce the finer points of obstruction. It is generally accepted that the natural stance of a netball player is in an upright position with knees and elbows slightly flexed. Players with-

PRACTICE EXAMPLE

In a group of four, players have the roles of Player 1, Player 2, an umpire (with a whistle and a 0.9m measure) and a feeder. Players 1 and 2 stand back-to-back 0.5m apart with the feeder facing Player 1 standing 3–4m away. A cone is placed 2.5m opposite Player 2.

The umpire blows the whistle and the feeder passes the ball to Player 1. At the same time Player 2 runs forward around the cone. Player 1 turns round to face the direction of Player 2. Player 2 takes up a position of what they think is 0.9m. The umpire will either let Player 2 defend or blow the whistle immediately to penalize the obstruction. The umpire can check the decision with the 0.9m measure. Each member will rotate through the different roles.

This drill can be progressed with Player 1 attempting an imaginary shot at goal with Player 2 jumping upwards or toward Player 1 from a starting distance of 0.9m. This will also help players to judge their timing when intercepting a shot.

out the ball are deemed to be obstructing if they are defending an opponent with their arms away from their body. When moving around the court, players should be coached to have their arms close to the body but ready to receive a pass. At the point at which the pass is made players can attempt to catch or intercept the pass with their arms away from the body. They can also momentarily signal for a pass, indicate where they are going to move or want a pass fed to.

Players can be within 0.9 metres of an opponent with the ball as long as they are not attempting to intercept or defend the ball or interfere with the throwing or shooting action of that player. This is particularly important when players are defending an opponent taking a shot. If a player defends the shot with outstretched arms and falls forward they can be coached to bring their hands down before they ground their foot/feet within 0.9 metres. As long as the action does not interfere with

the shooting or throwing action of their opponent, the umpire should allow this.

Coaches should make players aware that 'intimidation' is any action that may be used to give an unfair advantage to a player or team. This includes waving or pointing at the face and placing hands in front of the eyes. These actions are particularly apparent when players are defending a shot at goal. Coaches should be proactive when it comes to this scenario and instruct players to mark the ball and aim to place the hand over the ball in a fixed position avoiding the eyes.

Contact

In the early stages of learning the core netball rules, young players need to be coached that they cannot come into contact with an opponent either accidentally or deliberately. They are also not permitted to place their hands on a

Players should develop an understanding of the 0.9 metre distance that is adopted when defending a player with the ball.

ball which is held by another player. As the skill level increases, the concepts of 'contest' and 'interference' should be introduced. Umpires will continually assess whether any contact that occurs has interfered with a player's ability to make a successful pass or to take a shot.

When two players make contact with each other and it is a balanced action the umpire will consider this to be a contest. Contest can also occur when two players jump up for a ball and touch each other but it is balanced and fair and neither player has interfered with the playing action of the other. Umpires who judge contact to have interfered will either penalize the offending player with a penalty pass or penalty shot or choose to play advantage. Coaches should ensure that players know that the whistle indicates that play is required to stop but when umpires call 'advantage' they want play to continue. Young players often

stop when an umpire calls advantage as they are unsure if a decision has been made.

Throw-In

A throw-in may seem like a straightforward action but players will need to be aware of some finer points concerning it. When the ball goes out of court the throw-in is put back into play by a member of the opposing team. Players taking the throw-in must make sure that all other players are on court at the time they take the throw-in and that they place one or both of their feet immediately behind the point where the ball crossed the line. Players taking throw-ins must observe the footwork rule, throw the ball within 3 seconds and not enter the court until the ball has been thrown.

Players of all abilities are often unsure of how close to position their foot/feet to the

A player here supports the coach by taking a lead on decisions related to the throw-in when the ball has gone out of court.

line without being penalized. As a general guide the foot/feet should be between 5 and 8 centimetres from the line. This will ensure that players do not roll their foot/feet forward onto the line when playing the ball. Players should also be reminded of the 'over a third' rule when taking a throw-in and that they may not step behind any offside area while still in possession of the ball. It would be advantageous to practise throw-ins during sessions with a number of scenarios.

Toss-Up

A toss-up very rarely occurs in the elite game; however, they do appear frequently within junior and youth netball matches. Coaches need to educate players about the rules and procedures surrounding it.

A toss-up will occur following a number of simultaneous actions:

- Opposing players gaining simultaneous possession of the ball.
- Opposing players simultaneously knocking the ball out of court.
- Opposing players making simultaneous contact.
- Opposing players simultaneously offside, with one in possession of or touching the ball.

Practising the toss-up can be a fun addition to many coaching sessions, with players acting as umpires too.

Summary

The rules of netball can often provide barri-

ers to the development of skills due to their complexity and it is therefore vital that a coach introduces the technical skills alongside the related netball rules. The signals an umpire uses can also be introduced to promote greater levels of understanding and faster responses to umpire calls in a game. Introducing and integrating the rules as early as possible will give young players a good understanding, which can often lead to improved performances compared to those participants who have not received coaching with the rules embedded in a session. Where possible, young players should experience how to umpire in a coaching session and take on the role of the umpire in small-sided game situations. As confidence develops, players can begin to umpire the full court game with support from the coach.

TOSS-UP PRACTICE

Three players will assume the roles of Player 1, Player 2 and umpire. Player 1 and 2 stand facing each other. Their arms are by their sides but their feet can be in any position. There should be a distance of 0.9m between the nearer foot of each player. The players are required to stay in this position until the umpire blows the whistle. The umpire needs to release the ball midway between the two players from just below the shoulder level of the shorter player. The umpire holds the ball in the palm of one hand and flicks it vertically in the air as he or she blows the whistle. The player who takes possession of the ball is the winner. If both players take possession simultaneously it is deemed a draw and the toss-up is taken again. Each player should rotate through the roles.

CHAPTER 9

DEVELOPING PSYCHOLOGICAL SKILLS AND LEADERSHIP

Jane Lomax

Children and young people's reasons for playing netball are varied, and coaches play a vital role in meeting their needs so that players can enjoy their netball over the long term. As youngsters work their way through the different age groups from childhood through adolescence we know the impact of the peer group has an increasingly powerful effect on their participation in sport, and their status within that peer group can enhance their enjoyment of netball, or not. The quality of friendships gained during their netball and the extent to which each player feels they 'fit in' with others will directly impact on their developing image of themselves, or self-concept. Coaches have a unique opportunity to support their players through this challenging stage of their careers by paying attention to the psychological, personal and social development of players in addition to the technical, tactical and physical work (Haskins, 2010).

This chapter explores how coaches can develop confidence, a key mental skill in young players, to manage the challenges of competition and training as well as the social challenges faced. It explores integrating the development of leadership skills to encourage players to take on responsibilities and enhance their feelings of belonging, self-worth and mental toughness. Coaches are also encouraged to support players in their efforts to manage any anxiety they experience on the way.

Understanding Confidence

Confidence is about having the belief that we can succeed at a task we are presented with. Rather than being what we hope to do, it is what we realistically expect to do (Burton and Raedeke, 2008). Developing confidence is a long and gradual process (Woodlands, 2006), but once there, confident players perform better, experience higher levels of concentration, enjoy more positive emotions and, where this confidence is extended to the social elements, tend to fit in better with their peers and team-mates. Confident players tend to choose more challenging goals (Weinberg and Gould, 2011) and work harder to achieve them, and where this confidence can be built as a group the same will apply to the collective whole. Although some players will naturally be more confident than others, confidence always has the potential to desert us at any time, so it is well worth coaches taking time to reflect on individual differences and how best to adapt the coaching environment to support confidence growth.

Understanding Leadership

Despite the long-running debate as to whether good leaders are born or made, we do know that good leaders inspire, motivate and organize others; they manage change, set direction and have empathy (Whittaker, 2003). The value of these qualities, not just to the team but to the developing youngsters themselves, cannot be underestimated and coaches can assist in developing these qualities in their young players by modelling them and utilizing a range of coaching styles to provide opportunities to develop a sense of responsibility in players and give them an input into the direction their training is heading. Players who can develop empathy will be able to understand others, teammates and officials alike, which develops an appreciation of appropriate behaviour in training as well as under competition pressures. All of these can help maintain player confidence, and the ensuing positive atti-tude will help young players develop a sense of belonging and fitting in with their peers.

Sources of Confidence and Anxiety

Sources of confidence for players (Jones and Kingston, 2013; Hays, Maynard, Thomas, and Bawden, 2009; Vealey and Chase, 2008) include the following.

Within netball:

- Underlying abilities
- Working well with other players
- Netball knowledge

- Playing to the level of their peers
- Making good decisions from others
- Reacting to different opponents and game types
- Recovering from mistakes
- Coping with pressure
- Communication from coach
- Believing in coach's decisions and leadership

From outside netball:

- Fitting in with peer group
- Feelings of self-worth; body image
- Support from home
- Understanding expectations
- Balancing life, education and sport

Positive interpretation of these by players builds confidence nicely but it only takes a small shift in player perceptions of the situation to change those feelings of confidence to anxiety and players can start worrying about the very things that were previously giving them confidence. This is most likely to occur under the pressure of competition, particularly where the consequences of performance are high – for example, when under selection or moving up into a new team or age group. Confident players tend to experience lower levels of anxiety or, if they do get anxious, are better able to cope. Here is an overview of some helpful strategies.

Strategies to Develop Confidence and Leadership Skills

Many ideas for developing confidence in specific situations are drawn from Bandura's (1977) theory of 'Self Efficacy', which identifies the most important source of confidence as our previous successes, or performance accomplishments. Winning matches and gaining selection success give powerful messages to young players but these results are only partially under the youngsters' control. Coaches can go much further than this to build confidence by making sure their definition of 'success' goes beyond results alone. The acknowledgement and rewarding of effort levels and personal improvement to reinforce the importance of mastering new skills and standards of play can encourage players to focus on the intrinsic rewards of playing, which are more likely to keep young players in the sport long term than relying on results alone.

Coaches can use **goal setting** principles to help. Making sure the purpose of tasks within training sessions is specific and clearly outlined helps players know exactly what is expected of them and channels their concentration and effort levels. Improvements towards the goals are then clear to see for players and coaches, who have the opportunity to praise that progress. Coaches need to give players enough time to develop their expertise within practice tasks, and the practice structure and task progressions need to make it easy for players to see the relevance of training exercises to the game. Players need to be challenged and coaches need to be able to adapt each task to extend those who are picking up the work easily and simplify tasks for anyone who is struggling. Where the coach pitches tasks at the right level for players, they will be challenged but have the opportunity to experience success. It is this build-up of a bank of successes that steadily builds con-fidence.

Competition and match play encourage all of us to focus on outcome goals, i.e. beating the opposition. An over-emphasis on this by coaches, though, can make players' confidence levels very reliant upon whom they are playing next and tends to result in a roller-coaster of emotions that run high when the team wins but plummet when they lose. To stabilize this, coaches can underpin outcome goals with performance and process goals. These are the stepping stones towards the desired outcome and are progressively more under the players' control.

The coach clarifies her expectations of the task to ensure player success.

Performance goals – measurable aspects of performance to focus on, for example:

- Achieve six turnovers per quarter.
- 80 per cent of feeds from within 1 metre of the circle edge.

Process goals – these relate to the everyday focus on training or competition and are often the coaching points towards achieving a task. These goals are most under the players' control, for example:

- Drive to the top of the D.
- Pivot/turn to look for straight line ball down the court.

Using these stepping stones towards the desired outcome can help players know exactly what the coach expects of them. Coaches can individualize the goals to extend players according to their needs and allow them to reap the full benefits of their efforts. When coaches use this type of goal-setting within matches, there is more scope for evaluation after the game and players can have achieved some 'success' in their work whatever the result of the match. This stabilizes confidence levels and, if used over time, can provide individual step-by-step guidance for achieving long term ambitions (Navin, 2008).

Encouraging Players to Take Responsibility

Establishing a rapport and dialogue with the players helps coaches find out what motivates them and what their aspirations are. Coaches can then consider player interests within the planning of sessions and even share some of the goal-setting. Using a variety of coaching styles helps develop players' cogni-

tive, social and leadership skills, and including the following points will empower players:

- Set up problem-solving tasks.
- Give players responsibilities for elements of a session, e.g. reciprocal teaching, which helps develop each other's performance and integrate young players socially and morally (Jones and Standage, 2006).
- Create interaction with players by introducing tasks that need observation and giving of feedback and support. Less skilled players will gain much self-esteem and feelings of self-worth if they are able to help and advise a more skilful player (Telema and Polvi, 2007).
- Develop opportunities for more formal leadership roles – team captain is a popular choice. But consider whether this is a consistent role for one individual or whether the role should be rotated to allow more players to develop this skill

A young player is seen here giving feedback to two of her peers to assist the execution of a defensive task.

set. Perhaps the notion of 'captain' could be extended to units/court areas or even substitutes.

- Develop positive attitudes in the players by the coach demonstrating consideration and respect for players and expecting the same behaviour back. Encouraging players to be respectful to officials, each other and opposition players by shaking hands after matches and thanking people for their support are easy to achieve – though sincerity might need encouraging at times! This can be extended to develop understanding for officials and helping players adapt their game to manage differences of opinion over rule interpretations.

- Help to resolve conflict as it arises through the season. Developing cooperation between players who are in competition helps and increases enjoyment of the activity, develops communication and shares information (Weinberg and Gould, 2011). Information and goal-setting can be shared with parents too, particularly decisions in relation to selection and playing time, to keep channels of communication open.

To facilitate these positive dynamics, coaches need to adopt an approach where mistakes are a natural part of learning. This helps players accept responsibility for actions and works to develop growth from those mistakes. Coaches should emphasize the positive developments in performance rather than focusing on mistakes and what is missing. This develops a positive work ethic and leads to a mutually supportive environment. Coaches can also show respect and appreciation for player efforts and adopt an atmosphere that is disciplined and fair but positive and encouraging. Coaches losing their cool on the side line will not help achieve that!

Developing a Positive Mind-Set

Encouraging a focus on positive thoughts helps reduce the time players spend thinking negatively or talking themselves out of things. This can be **verbal persuasion** from the coach or others around the player, but coaches need to monitor this to ensure the 'persuasion' is both appropriate and positive. Where players need convincing that they are able to do something, coaches can identify players who are similarly experienced and have them successfully completing the task in order to encourage the player to mimic them. This is particularly useful when setting up demonstrations, and careful use of players here will give the rest of the group the oppor-

The coach allows players to explore solutions to defensive teamwork in the circle to steer the shooter and then call the front defender to intercept, and shooters explore how to play against the defensive strategy. Mistakes are seen as good learning opportunities.

The coach encourages the use of key words 'reach' for early Stage 2 defending skills, quickly followed by 'strong' to box out the rebound.

tunity to feel encouraged to try something by adopting a mind-set of 'if they can do it, so can I' (vicarious experience).

Players are often very good at talking to themselves and this can be helpful if harnessed productively. Sadly, many players tell themselves off or use their self-talk as a release for frustration, which often does little to improve confidence levels. Encouraging players to use key words when they are working to support their practice helps train **positive self-talk** (Mace, 1995). Examples might include:

- 'Plant – drive' to encourage a quick change of direction.
- 'Smooth', 'set' or 'breathe' when preparing to shoot.
- 'Mine' when going for an interception.

Where players experience negative self-talk, coaches can try to neutralize this or turn the negative statements into more positive ones (cognitive restructuring), as in Fig. 9.1.

Negative thoughts	Possible positive alternatives
'My opponent was really rough last match and she really put me off my shooting.'	'Hold my ground, stand tall, keep my cool and 'set' before shooting.'
'I must not go offside at the centre pass again or the coach will drop me.'	Think 'hold – whistle – go' at the next centre pass.
'That was a terrible feed. If I carry on like this it could cost us the match.'	'All players make mistakes. One missed pass will not lose a match. Lift the ball into the non-defender side of the shooter more next time.'

Fig. 9.1   Turning negative into positive.

Where players find it difficult to move directly from a negative thought to a positive one, introduce a **thought stopping** image. This could be thinking of a red light or raising your hand in a stop pose, or even saying 'stop' to yourself to break the negative thoughts. Then, if the player can move directly to a positive alternative, do so. If not, something neutral may help as a mediator; the use of key words is helpful here – 'quiet', 'calm', 'smooth' – to refocus the thinking onto something that might be more productive for confidence.

Players finding it difficult to change negative thoughts can try 'parking' or 'binning' them. Here an analogy that has worked well with players over a range of ages is the notion of **binning your baggage**. Players image a bin outside the training or match venue that they put all the thoughts bothering them into on arrival, thus freeing the mind to focus on the match or training at hand. When play has finished image a sieve part of the way down the bin – let those things that are no longer important sink through the sieve and be binned for good. Those that are important to address now need to be caught in the sieve, retrieved, and dealt with.

Use Imagery Skills – See and Feel Yourself Being Successful

Some players are naturally very good at picturing themselves playing; children have vivid imaginations and are often creative in their thinking. This is therefore an excellent time to use those talents. When players perform well or improve at a particular skill, encourage them to think this through again before their next turn. If they are able to picture themselves and feel the movements as well, that will be even more powerful. Encourage them to enjoy imaging themselves being successful so that when they are not having such a good day they can have a positive image to default to that can top up their confidence.

Confidence can also be boosted if players image themselves completing a task they are about to do before starting it. This may form part of a pre-match warm-up routine, or can be useful for shooters practising what they want to do next time they shoot, refocusing after a missed shot. Mentally practising tasks in this way speeds up the learning of new skills; coaches should encourage players to spend a few minutes mentally practising to support their physical practice attempts.

Exude Confidence – 'Walk Tall'

Players can send out powerful messages

The coach reinforces the positive attempts at keeping a roll dodge close to the opponent and encourages both players to mentally rehearse the movement before going back on court.

about their levels of confidence without real-izing it – by their posture, use of non-verbal messages and their behaviour. If negative, this can give the opposition the upper hand and, if negative vibes are given off as a substitute, can decrease selection possibilities. Encourage impression management, particularly after making mistakes – this can be as simple as lifting the shoulders, puffing out the chest a bit and 'walking tall'. It changes the whole impression given and can help players rebuild confidence from the outside, too. Use the '3Cs mind-set' and think 'Cool – Calm – Calculating'.

Team Confidence

Coaches can develop a sense of confidence that relates to the team as well as individuals. This is collective efficacy and is a more powerful indicator of team performance than summing up individual confidence levels. Coaches can encourage higher collective efficacy with the use of team goal-setting, which can be broken down into court unit goals and then individual contributions to those goals. This can help keep individual goals aligned with others and can assist coaches in their desire to have the whole team 'singing off the same page'. This is another opportunity for coaches to develop leadership skills as players can take responsibility for generating their unit goals and supporting their implementation.

Coaches can help players understand their role (Burton and Raedeke, 2008) and prepare them to fulfill it, ensuring that all roles are fully valued and goals are set realistically for each player. Players can be encouraged to 'Play with P.R.I.D.E.', i.e. their Personal Responsibility In Delivering Excellence. Successful teams are those where mutual trust between players has been developed so that they can to carry out their roles successfully, helped by a positive, supportive team environment and culture.

The coach agrees unit goals within a training game and helps clarify the role of each player.

Managing Anxiety

Confident players should be able to cope well with training and competition. Where confidence deserts them and they experience anxieties, the coach may need to help them manage these emotions.

Players can experience heightened physical symptoms – increased heart rate, sweaty palms, frequent toilet visits or feelings of nausea. These symptoms (somatic anxiety) tend to peak on arrival at a match venue, normally dissipating once performance starts, so a good warm-up before a match can help. If somatic anxiety reappears, though, it causes increased tension levels in the muscles, which

Breath control – taking deeper, slower breaths, perhaps coupled with counting to three or five slowly to encourage deep breaths and help calm the individual.

Tension control – tightness often first appears in the neck and shoulders, which will quickly affect performance. If participants can be encouraged to step back from the activity and take control of rising tension, this can be checked at a manageable point. Training tension control in muscles can be helped with the simple exercise of lifting your shoulders up to your ears, tensing all the muscles as hard as you can, then releasing those muscles, letting the tension drain away from them.

affects the way players move. Movements become snatched, lose their fluidity and in extreme cases players may not be able to perform movements at all. Breath control and relaxation can help:

Players who 'worry' are experiencing cognitive anxiety and would benefit from using the positive mind-set examples given above to prevent the anxiety interfering with their concentration and causing decision-making errors. Coaches need to encourage positive interpretations of changes in physical and cognitive arousal levels and read them as the body being ready for action to avoid them

building to a point where they adversely affect performance.

Match Preparation – Getting Players 'In the Zone'

Players perform better when in an appropriate level of mental and physical alertness (arousal). A popular approach to ensuring players are physically and mentally ready for competition aims to get players in a 'zone' of readiness where they can perform well (Hanin, 1980). Fig. 9.2 illustrates how players are mentally tuned in and alert, physically ready and 'in control' of their actions and reactions.

Coaches need to recognize individual differences in the size of the 'zone' and thus the range of arousal levels a player can function well over. In Fig. 9.2, Player 1 has a wide range of arousal levels and is likely to be more flexible in performing under different situations; Player 2, however, only has a narrow band of arousal levels that she performs well under and may require more precise preparation for a match in order to play to her full potential. So coaches need to notice when each player is outside her 'zone' or heading in that direction, and help draw her back. This may include considering individual differences in when and how we intervene or give feedback as well as the nature and tone of pre-match talks, particularly with respect to the emotional content – for some players the worst thing a coach could possibly do is

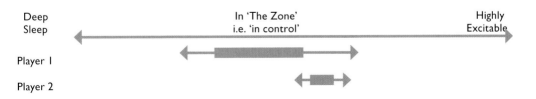

Fig. 9.2   Getting into the zone.

hype them up, but for others this strategy works well. To practise controlling arousal levels and maximizing the time players spend 'in the zone', the following strategies may help:

Summary

The key to any of the ideas suggested in this chapter rests in the communication skills of the coach. The empathy coaches have for their players' efforts and the management of pressures that are a natural part of competitive sport will develop positive dynamics and confidence; a less empathetic coach runs the risk of generating the opposite! Leadership skills can be developed as an integral part of training and competing and will contribute to the development of confident players, who are able to cope better with anxieties and frustrations that are an inevitable part of development.

To psych players up when their arousal is too low:

- Use a thorough warm-up, maybe with some upbeat music playing.
- Use key words that stimulate effort – 'drive', 'mine', 'go'.
- Practise mentally what you are about to do.

To psych players down when their arousal levels are too high:

- A short, sharp burst of intense activity to get rid of excess emotions.
- Calm players down – maybe with calming music.
- Key words to calm – 'smooth', 'steady'.
- Remind yourselves of previous good performances.
- Rehearse what you are about to do.
- Breath control or relaxation.
- Keep things in perspective.

CHAPTER 10

NUTRITIONAL GUIDELINES
Penny Rumbould

Recent research has identified that 43 per cent of coaches (netball and hockey) would rate their knowledge on this topic as average despite providing regular nutritional advice to their players (Cockburn, Fortune, Briggs and Rumbold, 2014). It is particularly important for coaches who work with young athletes in a sport and/or exercise context to recognize that the underlying physiology of children is very different from that of adults. Thus, when prescribing nutritional advice, consideration must be given to young people's growth and maturation needs, their movement efficiency, metabolism and finally their ability to thermo-regulate.

Bearing in mind the underlying physiological differences between children and adults, therefore, and with an increasing amount of research suggesting coaches lack the correct nutritional knowledge (Cockburn et al., 2014), the aim of this chapter is to provide nutritional guidelines that netball coaches can use to support their young players. However, it must be recognized that there is not a 'one size fits all' nutritional outline and that coaches should make informed decisions when advising individual athletes.

The Training Diet

Unlike for adult athletes, the main aim of a nutritional programme for young play-ers is first and foremost to support growth and maturation. Once this is successfully achieved, nutritional methods to support and enhance performance can then be explored. Accordingly, the World Health Organization (2004) defines energy requirements in young athletes as 'the amount of food energy needed to balance energy expenditure in order to maintain body size, composition and a level of necessary and desirable physical activity consistent with long-term health. This includes the energy needed for optimal growth and development of children.'

Energy Needs

Most individuals maintain a stable body mass over long periods of time, with little attention paid to the amount they eat (through food) and the amount they expend (through exercise). For athletes, however, this is a more important consideration given the extra energy cost of their training. In addition, if the amount of energy used in training exceeds the energy eaten by the athlete, the ability to obtain other nutrients (carbohydrate, protein, iron and calcium) necessary for optimal performance and good health is compromised. Therefore, it is imperative for young athletes such as netball players to ensure they are in a state of energy balance, whereby the amount of energy consumed through food is adequate to meet the amount expended during training.

Indeed, recent research has identified that adolescent netball players (thirteen- to fifteen-year-olds) are in a state of energy deficit by at least 234 Kcal/d on rest days and 798 Kcal/d on match days (Rumbold, Gibson, Allsop, Stevenson and Dodd-Reynolds, 2011). Furthermore, the energy cost of growth (approximately 5 Kcal/g of body mass) (Millward, Garlick and Reeds, 1976) must also be considered, since during the pubertal growth spurt (between eight to ten years in girls) a slight positive energy balance is required where energy intake must exceed energy expended by 1–2 per cent (Livingstone and Robson, 2000). Furthermore, the energy cost of walking or running at any given speed, when calculated per kg body mass, is higher in children and adolescents compared to adults (Åstrand, 1952). Consequently, as a general rule for pre-pubertal players 25–30 per cent should be added onto their standard recommended energy needs and for adolescent players an extra 10–15 per cent.

Although focused around health preservation as opposed to sport/exercise demands, the Scientific Advisory Committee for Nutrition (2011) has published revised recommendations for energy intake in children and adolescents, taking into account both the energy cost of growth and elevated physical activity levels (see Table 10.1). Coaches may use these as a guide when counselling young players about their daily food intake.

Diet Composition

Children and adolescents have lower concentrations of certain enzymes that enable the body to use carbohydrate as a fuel during exercise compared to adults, while having elevated concentrations of other enzymes that enhance the use of fat as an energy source. Young athletes therefore rely less on carbohydrate as a fuel for exercise compared to adults. However, from a nutritional prescription perspective this information needs to be

Table 10.1 Energy intake recommendations for girls aged seven to eighteen years (adapted from the Scientific Advisory Committee for Nutrition, 2011).

Age (years)	Daily Energy Intake Recommendations (Kcal/d)		
	Less Active	Average	More Active
7	1,386	1,529	1,648
8	1,481	1,624	1,768
9	1,553	1,720	1,863
10	1,863	1,935	2,054
11	1,935	2,031	2,150
12	2,031	2,102	2,246
13	2,150	2,222	2,389
14	2,246	2,341	2,484
15	2,293	2,389	2,532
16	2,317	2,413	2,580
17	2,341	2,461	2,604
18	2,365	2,461	2,628

applied with caution. High fat diets are not conducive to optimal training and performance in young athletes and have implications for health problems later in life. Furthermore, high fat intakes make it difficult to achieve adequate carbohydrate intake. Therefore, despite children's greater reliance on fat as fuel, elevated fat intakes are not advocated for the above reasons. Unlike carbohydrate and fat, protein contributes minimally to fuelling exercise, but instead is important for growth and development of body organs and tissues in young people as well as promoting recovery of muscle following exercise.

Consequently, it is suggested that young athletes should be consuming carbohydrate, protein and fat in daily proportions of 55 per cent, 12–15 per cent and 30 per cent respectively. Indeed, recent research in female adolescent netball players has identified that their daily diet on a match day was comprised of ~65 per cent carbohydrate, ~16 per cent protein and ~19 per cent fat (Rumbold et al., 2011).

Carbohydrate Requirements

Unfortunately, there is no specific child data that can be used by coaches to provide advice on carbohydrate requirements to support exercise. Although there is a tendency towards increased fat use during exercise in young people, prolonged bouts of netball training and high intensity explosive bouts of exercise, which frequently occur in netball, still require adequate stores of carbohy-

Players should be reminded regularly about the need for a balanced diet. Explosive bouts of exercise require adequate stores of carbohydrate.

Table 10.2 Recommended daily carbohydrate intake (adapted from Burke and Deakin, 2010).

Scenario		Carbohydrate Targets (g/kg/d)
Light	Low-intensity/skill-based activities	3–5
Moderate	Moderate exercise programme (~1h/d)	5–7
High	Endurance programme (moderate–high intensity exercise 1–3h/d)	6–10
Very High	Extreme commitment (moderate–high intensity exercise >4–5h/d)	8–12

drate, not only to support performance but also health. Therefore, coaches working with young players should ensure adequate carbohydrate reserves are maintained by using the adult-based carbohydrate requirements, which prescribe carbohydrate based on an individual's body mass and training load (frequency, intensity and duration).

Considering that young athletes rely less on carbohydrate as a fuel for exercise compared to adults, the values in Table 10.2 should be adjusted accordingly. Given the greater capacity for fat use in pre-pubertal children it is likely carbohydrate stores are conserved, which in turn may reduce the requirement for increased dietary carbohydrate. Furthermore, carbohydrate intake should be altered on a daily basis to map training load (i.e. on high exercise days players may require 6–10g/kg/d of carbohydrate; however, if the session is more skills-based the following day this should be reduced to 3–5g/kg/d). For example, a 50kg player would require 300–500g of carbohydrate on high exercise days and 150–250g of carbohydrate on skills-based days.

Protein Requirements

For adults, adequate protein intake is defined as the minimal amount needed to maintain nitrogen balance. In contrast, children and adolescents must maintain a positive nitrogen balance (i.e. protein intake must be higher than the amount used) for the purpose of growth and development of body organs and tissues, despite there being no difference in metabolism between adults and children with regards to protein. Therefore the increased protein requirements of children compared to adults refer not to poor utilization, but to growth and exercise needs. It is recommended that children aged seven to ten years consume 1.1–1.2g/kg/d and children aged eleven to fourteen years take 1.0g/kg/d (Ziegler et al., 1998). Research indicates that protein intakes are above recommended levels in young athletes, even in sports such as gymnastics where energy intake is often reported as being restricted.

Other Nutrients

Iron

Female adolescents undertaking hard training have a higher requirement and turnover of iron, which can quickly deplete iron stores. A decrease in performance capacity and recovery is related to the function of iron and its role in oxygen transport.

The Health Survey for England recommends that iron consumption for girls aged seven to ten years should equate to 8.7mg/d (e.g. 85g of beef + 85g of turkey + one cup of cooked beans + one cup of pasta) and for older girls aged eleven to eighteen years this should be increased to 14.8mg/d by adding the following foods to the above (for example, one stalk of broccoli + one jacket potato + one cup of dried apricots).

It is useful for coaches to have some practical nutritional knowledge about how to lower the risk of their players becoming iron deficient. Such information can then be discussed with the players themselves and parents/guardians if there is reason for concern.

Lower the risk of players becoming iron deficient by advising them to:

- Avoid low energy diets (less than 2,000 Kcal a day).
- Avoid very high carbohydrate diets (due to low bioavailability of iron from some carbohydrate-rich foods, e.g. cereal and bread).
- Avoid irregular or erratic eating patterns.
- Consume vegetable-rich sources of iron (e.g. spinach) with orange juice (as vitamin C helps absorption).
- Avoid excessive consumption of tea or coffee with meals.
- Eat red meats, liver or shellfish three to five times per week.

Calcium

Calcium requirements are higher in young children, especially during the adolescent growth spurt, which typically occurs between eight to ten years in girls. Calcium affects bone growth and metabolism, tooth structure, and nerve and muscle function. Moreover, female athletes who have irregular menstrual periods also require extra calcium.

The Health Survey for England recommends that calcium consumption for girls aged seven to ten years should equate to 550mg/d (e.g. 150ml low fat fruit yoghurt + 150ml reduced fat milk + 66g almonds) and for older girls aged eleven to eighteen years this should be increased to 800mg/d (e.g. 250ml low fat fruit yoghurt + 250ml reduced fat milk + 66g almonds). Coaches should therefore encourage the intake of four to five servings per day of dairy products and/or fish with bones (e.g. tinned salmon, sardines).

Preparation for Competition

Netball is a high-intensity, repeated-sprint team sport, and therefore requires power, strength and endurance to maintain a high level of performance. Consequently, the aims of a pre-match meal are (a) to continue to fuel muscle glycogen stores if players have not fully recovered from the last training session, (b) restore liver glycogen content, especially for training/matches undertaken in the morning, and (c) ensure young athletes are well hydrated. Nutritional preparation for competition is therefore important to prevent fatigue due to energy depletion and dehydration, which impact on power, speed and strength generation.

Pre-Match Meal
Similar to daily carbohydrate recommended intakes, there is no specific child data regarding the optimal amount of carbohydrate that should be provided in the pre-event

meal. In adults it is suggested that a pre-match meal should be high in carbohydrate and low in fat, fibre and protein. Thus researchers have suggested that young athletes should experiment with increasing levels of carbohydrate in their daily diet leading up to matches to establish how performance is influenced. Levels should continue to be increased if no negative effects are identified. This meal should be consumed one to four hours pre-training or match. Most importantly, the nutritional strategies implemented by players prior to competition must be 'tried and tested' prior to training sessions.

PRE-MATCH MEAL IDEAS

- Breakfast cereal* with milk or yoghurt.
- Cereal bars or breakfast bars with juice or sports drink.
- Toast* with jam.
- Crumpets* with honey.
- Bread rolls* with banana.
- Liquid meal supplements – good if nervous before competition or if players experience gastrointestinal discomfort.
- Pasta* with tomato/low-fat sauces.
- Steamed rice*/noodle* with low-fat sauces.

*   choose 'white' types, not wholemeal (high fibre)

Adapted from Maughan & Burke, 2002.

Furthermore, coaches might identify players who seem fatigued during netball matches, despite adopting the above pre-match meal strategies. Preventative actions for coaches to use include:

- Advising players to experiment with timings and amounts of carbohydrate intake prior to exercise.
- Advising players to consume low glycaemic index foods (e.g. apple, nuts, yogurt) before exercise, to provide a slow release of glucose.
- Conducting a high-intensity warm-up – this will stimulate the release of glucose from the liver, preventing blood glucose levels from dropping too low.
- Advising players to consume carbohydrate throughout exercise where possible.

During Competition

During competition there are two nutritional considerations which come hand-in-hand: (a) ensuring players are taking on board enough carbohydrate to support performance, and (b) ensuring players are adequately hydrated.

An important consideration when working with young athletes is to recognize that their thermo-regulatory ability is a lot poorer compared to that of adults. Coupled with the fact that children's thirst mechanism underestimates actual fluid requirements, the result is an excessive increase in core body temperature. To combat this, young people should drink sufficient amounts of fluid during exercise. However, they often don't drink enough, resulting in 'voluntary dehydration' (i.e. dehydration that occurs even when drinks are offered in excess). Coaches should therefore make every effort to prevent dehydration in young players.

Players should be educated about the benefits of being fully hydrated prior to training and matches and encouraged to develop their own rehydration practices during these events. Coaches can facilitate this by (a) ensuring players turn up to training and matches fully hydrated, and (b) thinking carefully about the positioning of players' drinks around the court during training and matches.

Regular hydration breaks must be taken in a session.

COACHES' HYDRATION TIPS

When?
Advise players to drink every 15–20 minutes or enforce drink breaks every 15–20 minutes.

How much?
Advise players to drink to thirst.

What?
Something flavoured – grape (no added sugar) has been shown to be particularly effective for rehydration purposes. If exercise is above 75 minutes, include carbohydrate.

Temperature?
Chill drinks to 10°C to encourage players to consume fluids.

Recovery Diet

The recovery diet is one of the most under-considered aspects of a young player's diet, yet the most imperative as recovery starts immediately after the cessation of exercise. Important aspects of recovery include: consuming adequate amounts of carbohydrate to replenish fuel stores following exercise; consuming adequate amounts of protein to promote muscle recovery; and ensuring players are fully hydrated after their training session or match.

Carbohydrate and Protein Intake Post-Match

The optimal time to consume carbohydrate following exercise is within the first 30 minutes of exercise cessation. This period of time is known as the 'window of opportunity' as the highest sustained rates of carbohydrate storage occur during this period. Therefore, coaches should encourage players to consume a high glycaemic index snack, for example bananas or raisins (50–100g or 1.0g/kg), within 30 minutes of exercise cessation to promote optimal recovery.

Furthermore, some studies have identified that the addition of protein to recovery snacks enables the restoration of muscle glycogen stores even quicker than providing carbohydrate alone. Indeed, one such food/drink source that is gaining a lot of attention in promoting recovery following exercise is chocolate milk (Cockburn, Hayes, French, Stevenson and St Clair Gibson, 2008; Thomas, Morris and Stevenson, 2009). Players should therefore be encouraged to consume 10–20g or 0.5g/kg of protein following training and matches to promote optimal recovery.

Hydration

A simple yet effective means of establishing if young players have taken on board enough fluid during training and matches is to weigh each player before and after. The resulting change in body weight corresponds with fluid loss, i.e. 1g of weight loss equates to 1ml of fluid loss (1kg = 1L). Coaches can use this technique to establish the hydration status of their players and it will enable them to calculate how much fluid is required following training and matches to replenish fluid losses.

Another pertinent issue surrounding re-

COACHES' RECOVERY TIPS

Encourage players to eat 1.0g/kg of carbohydrate (50–100g) and 0.5g/kg protein (20g) within the first 20 minutes following netball training or competition. Recovery snacks providing ~50g carbohydrate and 20g protein include:

- Snack 1: Banana, 200ml fruit smoothie, Müllerlight yogurt, handful of nuts/seeds.
- Snack 2: 4 tbsp peanut butter, 2 slices of thick bread (white/brown).
- Snack 3: 30g raisins (mini packets), Müllerlight yogurt, handful of nuts/seeds.
- Snack 4: Nutrigrain oat baked bar, 400g milkshake (skimmed milk).
- Snack 5: 50g malt loaf, 400g milkshake (skimmed milk).
- Snack 6: 400g fresh fruit snack box (Tesco), Müllerlight yogurt.

Encourage the combination of recovery snacks with fluid to replace water and electrolyte losses; if logistically possible, players should be encouraged to consume skimmed milk after netball.

Encourage players to eat a mixed meal containing complex carbohydrates and protein as soon as possible (within two hours of the recovery snacks).

hydration in young people following exercise is which recovery beverage to advise. Recent research in children has identified skimmed milk to be better than water and the equivalent to carbohydrate-based sports drinks at promoting rehydration following exercise (Volterman, Obeid, Wilk and Timmons, 2012).

CHAPTER 11

COACH DEVELOPMENT
Abbe Brady and Barbara Daniels

This chapter introduces a number of topics central to the learning and development of netball coaches. The opening section invites coaches to consider the many sources of learning available and their own role in their development as coaches. Experiential learning is presented as a wonderfully diverse and rich medium through which coaches can engage in intentional practice and reflection to acquire new knowledge and skills. The concept of life-long learning is presented to remind us of the on-going opportunities and character-istics of effective learning for coaches regard-less of age, career stage or coaching context. The second half of the chapter introduces the concepts of fixed and growth mind-sets and the significant implications of these on a coach's practice, learning and development.

Types of Learning for Coaches

Learning can occur in many different contexts and in ways that may help different coaches at different times. There are requirements for coaches to gain minimum standard national governing body (NGB) qualifications in order to coach people in club and school environ-ments, and some coaches will wish to gain further qualifications to gain more expertise and/or to coach at different levels of perform-ance. Netball-specific and cross-sport work-shops are usually shorter than qualification courses and focus on sharing good practice or on specific coaching topics or skills.

Formal NGB qualifications and **non-formal** short courses or workshops offer opportunities for coaches to gain specific knowledge and information about technical skills and tactical approaches, and/or they may explore the wider processes of coaching that include the emotional, social and psychological welfare of players. In more recent times there has been an increasing focus on the specific needs of players of different ages and stages, enabling coaches to consider the differing needs of children, young people and adults.

Qualification courses and short courses are a good source of up-to-date guidance for coaches. As well as the information on offer, these events enable coaches to mix with others and share issues, strategies and successes. They are sometimes referred to as **mediated** learning environments (Moon, 2004), where someone else has a role to help you learn. However, the embedding of coach-ing knowledge, techniques and strategies inevitably happens away from these courses, where coaches learn through applying, prac-tising and refining new information and skills. So a key question is: 'How can coaches make the most of opportunities to learn from their day-to-day coaching and make the best use of formal qualification events when they attend them?'

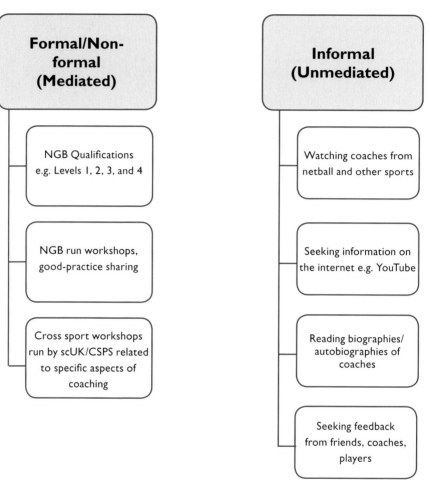

Fig. 11.1   Examples of types of learning opportunities for coaches.

Netball coaches have access to a rich variety of learning opportunities through the experiences they have in their own coaching environments and in the connections they make to other spheres in which they operate. These opportunities are known as **informal** or **unmediated** sources of learning and everyone has access to these. Most netball coaches will not be full-time coaches and will have experience and expertise that can inform their coaching. For example, many

coaches may be parents, former or current players of netball and/or other sports, or they may be teachers, their jobs may involve them in understanding people, building teams, developing communication skills, using technology and IT and many other things that will enable them to bring highly developed skills to coaching, even if they are 'beginners' in netball coaching (see Fig. 11.1).

What existing knowledge and skills do you bring to your netball coaching? Are there any others that you could utilize? What experiences have you had as a player of netball or other sports that may help you in understanding the different needs of the variety of players you may have at your club? In your home or work environment, what are you recognized as being good at? Are you known for your organization skills, ability to listen, or for engaging young people in activity to get them working together, for instance? This connection between your different environments and the ability to recognize and build on your experiences and skills is helpful in making the most of the many learning opportunities with which you are pre-sented.

Combining mediated (formal/non-formal), unmediated (informal) and self-reflective learning environments and processes is recommended as a powerful way for coaches to manage their own learning (Trudel, Culver

Self-reflection is an important tool for learning.

HOW CAN YOU LOOK AT WHAT YOU CURRENTLY DO AS A COACH?

You can begin simply by looking at the overview of coaching skills in the introduction and noticing what you do in each of these areas. You can supplement this by using video or audio, available on most smartphones, to capture yourself at different stages of a session and with different groups of players. Many coaches have never seen themselves 'in action' and it can be really enlightening to see what you actually do and what others see. Many people find it very helpful to discuss this with someone else who knows them and their coaching. You may wish to join up with one or two other coaches to help each other gain a clearer view of your coaching. These people are sometimes called coaching buddies.

and Werthner, 2013). Coaches who develop self-reflective processes and use the people around them to help and provide more rounded feedback about their coaching are better placed to manage their own development. Reflecting on one's coaching behaviour is linked to accelerated learning. Being aware of their own development needs will help coaches seek out and prioritize learning opportunities in their everyday coaching. This is referred to as experiential learning.

The Benefits of Experiential Learning

As coaches spend more time living their lives and working with players than they do on any courses, the ability to learn from experience is crucial if coaches are to continue to develop and build on what they gain from the more formal environments. One of the key benefits of this type of learning is that it can really take place anywhere and at any time, and often at no cost, if coaches are prepared to notice and make sense of what they see and do. So, what can coaches do in order to use their own experiences inside and outside netball to help focus their own development?

A good place to start is by looking at what you do currently. Build up a more detailed picture of how you behave, what the impact of your approach is, what your core values and beliefs are about coaching, where and when you are at your most confident as a coach, and where and when you are least confident.

How can you build a profile of what you think are your coaching strengths and of the areas that you might like to improve? Fig. 11.2 shows an example of a coaching profile approach.

Decide which areas you wish to focus on first in order to develop further. Be careful to pick only one or two to start with.

HOW CAN YOU BUILD A PROFILE OF YOUR COACHING STRENGTHS AND AREAS TO IMPROVE?

Look at the overview of coaching skills in this book and decide how you would rate yourself under each heading. It may be helpful to have in mind coaches you think are particularly good at certain coaching skills and rate yourself in comparison to them. Ask other coaches, parents and players for feedback about how they would describe your coaching and what they think are your strengths and the areas to develop. Remember to be open-minded and to accept that others may see you differently from how you see yourself. They may point out areas to develop that you haven't yet noticed; equally they may see strengths in you about which you are not yet aware.

Share these with your coaching buddies and ideally with a more experienced coach, too. Observe other coaches working and see if you can notice what they do really well. How do they manage to build good relationships with players? Be fair but fun? Be so organized? Have young players wanting to keep coming back? Be so patient?

HOW CAN YOU LEARN FROM OTHER COACHES?

Watch other coaches at your club, coaches at netball tournaments, coaches of other sports who you may see when you take your children to sports clubs, people who coach you in netball or other sports, your gym instructor(s), school PE teachers. Find out if any of your friends coach other sports and ask if you can watch; they may return the favour too. When you choose to notice, you can find coaching and other related skills happening all around you.

This approach will help you choose particular areas to focus on and to develop, so you can make the learning opportunity as big or as small as is appropriate. The opportunities will be incremental and will help you build a pattern of self-observation and reflection – supplemented by input from individuals whom you invite to help – on coaching skills that you have chosen, when you are ready to accept the challenge. Some people find it helpful to jot down brief notes so they don't forget their thinking and the feedback they are receiving. Some choose to audio record their thinking on their mobile phones so that they can listen back when they have the time. You will find ways that work for you and fit your

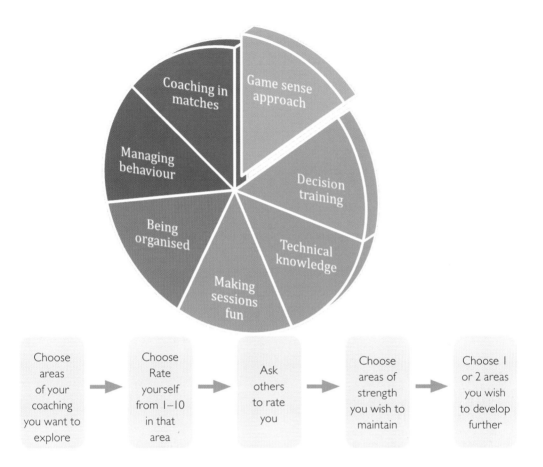

Fig. 11.2   Building your coaching profile.

life. It is also really important to notice and acknowledge all the good things that you do and that others see in you. Sometimes when you are looking to improve it is easy to lose sight of the strengths you are already bringing to your netball coaching.

When you do choose to go on further formal training, you will be in a better position to make the most of the inputs there and apply the most relevant to your coaching processes. There will also be opportunities to build networks with other coaches and to be open to experimentation and feedback. You can be proactive in this by being the person who sets up the Facebook page or Twitter group, or simply by asking one or two other coaches who live near you if you can go and watch them. This then allows you to take the formal learning opportunity directly into your own environment.

Experiential learning, therefore, is in your own hands! It happens at a pace to suit you, in the environments within which you coach and through the networks you build. With a little thought and planning it can be built into your life when it suits you and it can be a powerful way to develop. It helps to involve other people so you keep an all-round perspective and means that you will create a network of people who will help you celebrate the successes and cope with the disappointments and difficulties of being a coach. You may even find that an approach like this can help in other areas of your life, too.

The Development of Life-Long Learning Behaviours

As well as allowing us to stay involved in the sport we love and connected to people we like, being a netball coach provides us with on-going excitement, challenges and oppor-

tunities to learn and develop throughout our adult life. In this sense, netball coaching can be viewed as a valuable activity contributing to our life-long learning. Improving knowledge, skills and competence across all spheres and stages of life is now viewed as crucial because it provides people with tools for personal development, social integration and partici-pation in a rapidly evolving society (European Commission, 2006). The content, mode and location of learning will vary depending on the coach and his or her particular learning needs. Since coaches have a key role in direct-ing their own learning journey, it is important they recognize characteristics associated with thriving as effective life-long learners. These characteristics are diverse and include many

Observing and supporting other coaches is a powerful form of learning.

competencies, skills and attributes (see Fig 11.3).

Characteristics associated with effective life-long learning:

- Openness to experience and open-mindedness are essential attributes for life-long learning. These qualities are considered so important for human development that they feature in contemporary personality tests. Openness to experience is when people show they are prepared to try new things, are curious, imaginative and embrace variety. Coaches who do not display this tend to be more conservative in their learning and behaviours; they favour routine and avoid the new or unfamiliar, preferring traditional methods. The attribute of open-mindedness describes the coach who is interested in the views of others and values new or alternative ideas. Being open-minded is especially important when we work in teams and it is also linked to our creativity, reflexivity and adaptation.
- Cultivating self-awareness and reflexivity is important for effective life-long learning, because through purposeful and constructive reflection we can become more aware of our own strengths and learning needs as well as our preferences for how we best learn. This awareness helps us become more effective at judging our own competence and learning needs and, in turn, it informs the development opportunities we pursue.
- Adaptability and resilience are vital features of life-long learning as a coach, since an inevitable feature of developing coaching competence and knowledge is that it can be challenging and difficult at times. Facing obstacles or finding things more difficult than expected may test our belief about our capability and our moti-

Fig. 11.3   Characteristics of life-long learners

vation. Hence, important qualities we can all develop as coaches include becoming adaptive and resilient, which allow us to learn and respond appropriately in a range of situations, including when facing setbacks. People's capacity for adaptation and resilience is closely linked to their beliefs about their ability and learning possibilities (covered in the next section).

The Importance of a Growth Mind-Set

The concept of mind-set was introduced by Carol Dweck (2006). Mind-set is one of the most impactful contemporary topics to emerge in recent years and it's valuable for coaches across all settings and particularly for coaches of children. Dweck (2006) introduced mind-set to explain how individuals' beliefs about their intelligence and ability can influence how they view achievement and success, with significant consequences for motivation and persistence in learning. The two types of mind-set (growth and fixed) have distinct characteristics and can result in quite different interpretations about the value of activities and opportunities to develop. Having a growth or a fixed mind-set has considerable implications for qualities associated with effective life-long learning, such as openness to experience, self-aware-ness, reflexivity, adaptability and resilience. Most of the literature in sport has examined participants' mind-sets and yet the coach's mind-set is at least as crucial to consider, with significant implications for both the coach's own development and the players' experi-ence, too.

Netball coaches with a growth mind-set believe that, with time, guidance, purpose-ful practice and above all effort, they can develop their coaching ability through expe-riential learning. By contrast, netball coaches with a fixed mind-set believe real coaching ability is something you can't really develop that much because you either have or do not have what it takes to be a good coach. As a consequence, the coach with the fixed mind-set may believe that effort and practice are less important if one wants to become a successful netball coach. The coach with a fixed mind-set might think or say out loud that some players or coaches have 'natural ability' and great coaches and leaders are born not made or have a particular type of personal-ity. This type of coach might praise 'gifted-ness', 'natural talent' and winning, which may communicate that effort and persistence are less important. Coaches with a fixed mind-set might knowingly or unknowingly convey such ability beliefs to players and, in turn, this can encourage players to also adopt charac-teristics of a fixed mind-set. As we'll see in the following examples, a fixed mind-set is not desirable if we want coaches to motivate play-ers and also maximize their own enjoyment and thrive as netball coaches engaged in life-long learning.

Linked to beliefs consistent with their mind-set, coaches with a fixed or growth mind-set interpret things differently because in any given situation they are primed to notice particular things and make sense of the situation in a particular way. For example, an opportunity arises on a coach education course to demonstrate a personally designed netball practice with progressions to isolate a young player's throwing accuracy at pace. This may be interpreted by coaches with a growth mind-set as a useful activity to get some personal feedback and develop the practice for use with their own players. Fixed mind-set coaches may see the activity as one where they could make mistakes and their faults could be highlighted in front of the other coaches and coach educators. Which interpretation do you feel would be the most pleasant to expe-rience, make the task seem appealing, and be more likely to facilitate learning? Which coach might be most enthusiastic about taking the opportunity to demonstrate this practice and most likely to volunteer to do so? So here we can see how a particular mind-set might actually encourage or discourage coaches from taking an opportunity to learn for fear of others' judgements about their ability. We can see this same behaviour in our players, too.

When coaches with fixed and growth mind-sets experience success and failure, we can often see marked differences in their interpretations and consequent behaviours. When their teams win a match, coaches with a fixed mind-set might view it as especially satisfying when their players look far supe-rior, do not have to work too hard and make few mistakes. Coaches may see this success as confirmation of their coaching ability and/or their players' ability. This coach may have such a high regard for winning that players who are deemed less able may get little or no playing time. By contrast, the coach with a growth mind-set will be most satisfied if when the team win (or lose) the players have all tried their hardest, displayed good team work and risked trying the new marking strategy they've been working on. Coaches like this feel most satisfied when they see the children learning and developing as rounded young players, whether or not they win.

Even though we may sometimes meticulously plan training sessions, things do not always go as we'd hoped. When facing disruptions or failure, the fixed and growth mind-set coaches often respond in very different ways. Here's an example. The coach is trying to help young players learn two different strategies for moving the ball in and out of the circle to improve shooting position, and yet the practice repeatedly breaks down. The growth mind-set coach is patient and sees the situation as a learning opportunity by considering, 'What do I need to do or ask to help the players understand the practice?' The fixed mind-set coach might feel demoralized and see the situation as a problem with the players' concentration or motivation, or with the coach's own ability to teach the practice. These coaches may say to themselves, 'Why isn't this working? Whose fault is it?' These differences in thinking occur because coaches with growth or fixed mind-sets see failure very differently. Coaches with a growth mind-set may still be disappointed if their team do not win a match or if a practice session didn't go well, but they see failure in perspective, as an opportunity or even a wake-up call about the need to reflect, try harder, seek support and maybe change things. Failure for fixed mind-set coaches threatens their self-esteem; it may make them angry, they may blame others, avoid that practice in future and even withdraw altogether. Perhaps you have already seen examples of this in coaches (or players).

Netball coaches with a growth mind-set are motivated by different things compared to those with a fixed mind-set. Growth mind-set coaches set themselves (and their players) hard but realistic developmental challenges; goals set are personally referenced, meaning the coach's developmental goals are not about being better than other coaches, but better in relation to personal priorities or standards. Coaches with a growth mind-set see the bigger picture and so they are patient, they have a good sense of their present capability, show more self-compassion and look to support others (coaches and players) to do the same. As you can imagine, because coaches with a fixed mind-set believe their intelligence and ability are not open to much change, they are motivated in quite different ways. These coaches tend to set easier or unrealistic goals; they avoid situations where they could risk failing (often rich learning opportunities) or they compare themselves to others to determine progress/success. Fixed mind-set coaches want immediate results and consequently they tend to seek quick fixes to problems, rather than taking time to improve gradually. Knock-backs are highly demotivating and threaten these coaches' ability judgements. Fixed mind-set coaches may experience despair or choose to ignore instances when they receive critical feedback as this is viewed as personally demeaning. In contrast, even though they may be disappointed at first, coaches with a growth mind-set view setbacks as an opportunity to learn. Compared to those with a fixed mind-set, those with a growth mind-set may not get as upset about criticism because they appreciate that to really learn they have to try new things and that inevitably means making some mistakes along the way. Netball coaches with a growth mind-set are also more easily able to separate the critical feedback from their sense of self and their

Beliefs and behaviours of a coach with a growth mindset	Key concepts in a learning and development	Beliefs and behaviours of a coach with a fixed mindset
Doing one's best Trying hard Learning and improving Many types of success	Success	Establishing superiority with least effort Being gifted or a natural Success as winning
See the bigger picture Be patient Use self-referenced goals	Motivation	Want immediate results Seek quick fixes Compare self to others
Relish challenge and seek hard but realistic tasks	Challenges	Avoid challenge and seek easier or unrealistic tasks
See effort as investment – essential for learning and achievement	Effort	Not cool to show effort Effort needed by those struggling to achieve
Persist and find new ways	Obstacles	Become demotivated and distracted
View criticism as valuable feedback	Criticism	Ignore, dispute or denigrate criticism
Informative A wake up call Motivating	Failure	Ignore, dispute or denigrate criticism
Draw inspiration and ideas from others' success	Success of others	Ignore, dispute or denigrate criticism

view of their coaching ability. Hence coaches with a growth mind-set may be more resilient as learners precisely because they appreciate how developing as a coach takes time and effort. Though simplified, Fig. 11.4 summarizes the contrasting beliefs and behaviours in relation to coach learning and development associated with a growth or fixed mind-set.

Wow! What a difference mind-set can make to how netball coaches might think about their own learning and development! Imagine you are a young player – what type of coach mind-set would encourage you to most enjoy and thrive in netball? As a coach or player, can you recognize when you have adopted a fixed or growth mind-set? Do you notice certain situations when you tend to adopt a particular mind-set, and, if so, why is that?

Contemporary research into how knowledge, character strengths and abilities can be developed, as well as neuroscience findings about the on-going capacity of the brain to adapt and learn throughout the lifespan, support the value of adopting a growth mindset. It's helpful to think about mind-sets not as strict types or traits but as a style of thinking that can have powerful effects on our learning and development as coaches. Fortunately, we can all develop the features of a growth mind-set and here are some tips to make this happen.

This chapter has covered a wide range of topics relating to coach development. As well as recognizing the many sources of coach learning, we hope that coaches also appreciate that formal coach education courses are just one – albeit a very helpful component – of a coach's developmental journey. Everyday coaching also offers coaches a wealth of

To help adopt a growth mind-set, netball coaches should:

- Recognize that we are all capable of substantial development as coaches (and players) and that the notion of 'natural talent' can often be counterproductive.
- Appreciate that with suitably directed effort, and in some cases support from others, most of us can substantially improve or alter our coaching knowledge, skills and competencies.
- View our mistakes and failures as an expected feature of learning and recognize that these may provide some of the most valuable feedback for on-going development.
- Try a small 'praise experiment' to show how important effort is in motivation. In training or a match situation, observe how players respond after you praise their effort rather than the outcome of an activity.
- Read Carol Dweck's book *Mindset: The new psychology of success* and view her 10-minute TedTalk entitled 'The power of believing that you can improve'.

opportunities for experiential learning, and harnessing some of these opportunities can dramatically accelerate a coach's development. With awareness of the many informal opportunities for learning and of the important attributes for effective life-long learning, coaches and especially those who adopt a growth mind-set will be empowered to discover learning opportunities and to guide their own rewarding learning journey.

OPPOSITE: Fig. 11.4 Characteristics of a growth mindset and a fixed mindset.

REFERENCES

Chapter 1

Côté, J. & Gilbert, W. (2009) An integrative definition of coaching effectiveness and expertise. *International Journal of Sports Science and Coaching*, 4, pp.307–323.

Edmondson, A.C. (2003) Speaking up in the operating room: How team leaders promote learning in interdisciplinary action teams. *Journal of Management Studies*, 40, pp.1419–1452.

Fraser-Thomas, J.L., Côté, J. & Deakin, J. (2005) Youth sport programs: An avenue to foster positive youth development. *Physical Education & Sport Pedagogy*, 10, pp.19–40.

Gould, D. & Carson, S. (2011) Young athletes perceptions of the relationship between coaching and developmental experiences. *International Journal of Coaching Science*, 5, pp.3–29.

Navin, A.L. (2013) *Skilled, Active and Qualified Coaches:* The Development of a Sport-specific Coaching System to Support the Participant Pathway Professional Doctorate Thesis, May 2013.

Petitpas, A. & France, T. (2010) Identity foreclosure in sport. pp282–291. In Hanrahan, S.J. & Anderson, M.B. (2010) *Routledge Handbook of Applied Sport Psychology:* New York, Routledge.

Chapter 2

Lerner, R.M. (2005) 'Promoting positive youth development: theoretical and empirical bases', Washington: National Research Council/Institute of Medicine, National Academies of Science.

Haskins, D., Jolly, S., Lara Bercial (2011) *A Coaching Children Curriculum, a Guide for Governing Bodies*. Sports Coach UK.

Useful information and links

Child Exploitation and Online Protection centre – www.ceop.police.uk

Think u Know – www.thinkuknow.co.uk – advice site for young people and parents NSPCC – Childline 0800 1111 – www.nspcc.org.uk

Child Protection in Sport Unit – www.nspcc.org.uk/inform/cpsu/cpsu_wda57648.html

Chapter 3

'Inclusion Spectrum' (Black and Haskins, 1996). in Bailey (2013) *Teaching Physical Education: A Handbook for Secondary School Teachers*, Routledge.

Chapter 4

Bunker, D. & Thorpe, R. (1982). A model for the teaching of games in secondary schools. *The Bulletin of Physical Education*, 18(1).

Chapter 9

Bandura, A. (1977) Self-Efficacy: Towards a unifying theory of behaviour change. *Psychological Review*, 84, pp.191–215.

Burton, D. and Raedeke, T.D. (2008) *Sport Psychology for Coaches*, Human Kinetics.

Hanin, Y. (1997) Emotions and Athletic Performance: Individual Zones of Optimal Functioning Model. *European Yearbook of Sport Psychology*, 1, 29–72.

Haskins, D (2010) *Coaching the Whole Child: Positive Development through Sport*. Coachwise Business Solutions.

Hays, K., Thomas, O., Maynard, I. and Bawden, M. (2009) The role of confidence in world-class sport performers. *Journal of Applied Sport Psychology*, 19. 434–456.

Jones, R.L. and Kingston, K. (Ed) (2013) *An Introduction to Sports Coaching Connecting Theory to Practice*. Routledge press 2nd Edition.

Mace, R . (1995) *With Netball in Mind*. Delmar Press Ltd.

Navin, A. (2008) *Netball Skills, Techniques, Tactics*. The Crowood Press.

Telema, R. and Polvi, S (2007) Facilitating Prosocial Behaviour and Physical Education in Liukkonen, J., Vereijken, B., Alfermann, D. and Theodorakis, Y. (Eds.) (2007) *Psychology for Physical Educators; Student in Focus*. Human Kinetics, 2nd Edition, pp. 85-100.

Vealey, R.S. and Chase, M.A. (2008) Self Confidence in Sport: conceptual and research advances. In T.S. Horn (Ed.) *Advances in Sport Psychology* Champaign, IL: Human Kinetics, 3rd Edition, pp.65–97.

Weinberg, R.S. and Gould, D. (2011) *Foundations of Sport and Exercise Psychology*. Human Kinetics 5th Edition.

Whittaker, D. (2003) The Coach as a Leader – Generating the Magic in the Space Between People. *Faster Higher Stronger*, Issue 19, April 2003, pp 6–8.

Woodlands, J. (2006) *The Netball Handbook: Winning essentials for players and coaches*. Human Kinetics

Chapter 10

Åstrand, P.-O. (1952). *Experimental studies of physical working capacity in relation to sex and age*. Copenhagen: Munksgaard.

Burke, L. and Deakin, V. (2010). *Clinical sports nutrition*. (Fourth ed.).

Cockburn, E., Fortune, A., Briggs, M. and Rumbold, P.L.S. (2014). Nutritional knowledge of UK coaches. *Nutrients*, 6, 1442-1453.

Cockburn, E., Hayes, P.R., French, D.N., Stevenson, E. and St Clair Gibson, A. (2008). Acute milk-based protein-CHO supplementation attenuates exercise-induced muscle damage. *Appl Physiol Nutr Metab*, 33(4), 775-783.

Livingstone, M.B.E. and Robson, P.J. (2000). *Measurement of dietary intake in children*. Paper presented at the Nutrition Society.

REFERENCES

Maughan, R. and Burke, L. (2002). Practical Strategies to Meet Goals. *Handbook of Sports Medicine and Science, Sport Nutrition* (p.148).

Millward, D.J., Garlick, P.J. and Reeds, P.J. (1976). The energy cost of growth. *Proceedings of the Nutrition Society*, 35, 339-349.

Rumbold, P.L.S., Gibson, A.S.C., Allsop, S., Stevenson, E. and Dodd-Reynolds, C. J. (2011). Energy intake and appetite following netball exercise over five days in trained 13–15 year old girls. *Appetite*, 56(3), 621-628.

Thomas, K., Morris, P. and Stevenson, E. (2009). Improved endurance capacity following chocolate milk consumption compared with two commercially available sport drinks. *Appl Physiol Nutr Metab*, 34(1), 78-82.

Volterman, K., Obeid, J., Wilk, B. and Timmons, B.W. (2012). Effect Of Milk Intake on Electrolyte Balance in Children After Exercise in the Heat. *Medicine and Science in Sports and Exercise*, 44, 580-580.

Ziegler, P. J., San Khoo, C., Kris-Etherton, P. M., Jonnalagadda, S. S., Sherr, B. and Nelson, J. A. (1998). Nutritional status of nationally ranked junior US figure skaters. *Journal of the American Dietetic Association*, 98(7), 809-811.

Chapter 11
Brady, A., & Hughes, S. (2013). *Exploring the impact of a best future-self intervention on the well-being of early career sport coaches: The mediating role of mindset.* Presentation at 3rd Biennial Meeting of the British Psychological Society's Division of Sport and Exercise Psychology, Manchester, UK.

Dweck, C. (2006). Mindset: *The new psychology of success.* NY: Random House.

Dweck, C. (2014). *The power of believing that you can improve.* Video on TedTalk Accessed 29.01.15. Available via http://www.ted.com/talks/carol_dweck_the_power_of_believing_that_you_can_improve

European Commission (2006). *Key competencies of lifelong learning.* Recommendation 2006/962/EC of the European Parliament and of the Council of 18 December 2006 [Official Journal L 394 of 30.12.2006]. Accessed 29.01.15. Available via http://eur-lex.europa.eu/legal-content/EN/TXT/?qid=1422709288712&uri=URISERV:c11090

Moon, J. (2004). *A Handbook of Reflective and Experiential Learning: Theory and Practice.* London: Routledge Falmer.

Trudel, P., Culver, D., & Werthner, P. (2013). Looking at coach development from the coach-learner's perspective: Considerations for coach administrators. In P. Potrac, W. Gilbert & J. Denison (Eds.), *Routledge Handbook of Sports Coaching* (pp. 375-387). London: Routledge.

INDEX

INDEX